54,-

P

'12

Innovations Lead to Economic Crises

Jon-Arild Johannessen

Innovations Lead to Economic Crises

Explaining the Bubble Economy

palgrave
macmillan

MÄNGELEXEMPLAR

Jon-Arild Johannessen
Kristiania University College and Nord University
Oslo/Bodø, Norway

ISBN 978-3-319-41792-9   ISBN 978-3-319-41793-6   (eBook)
DOI 10.1007/978-3-319-41793-6

Library of Congress Control Number: 2016957739

Cover illustration: © Andrew Paterson / Alamy Stock Photo

Printed on acid-free paper

This Palgrave Macmillan imprint is published by Springer Nature
The registered company is Springer International Publishing AG
The registered company address is: Gewerbestrasse 11, 6330 Cham, Switzerland

Preface

The investigation between innovation and economic crises is here based upon a systemic philosophy of history. A systemic philosophy of history, not systems philosophy, is to my knowledge new in the study of economic history.[1] As such, this is an innovation into the study of history. In the systemic philosophy of history, we try to uncover patterns and patterns which connect in the long run. Six economic crises are investigated in order to find a pattern between innovation and economic crises.

---

[1] Johannessen (2012)

Acknowledgements

I want to thank Assistant Professor Siri Hopland, Kristiania University College, Norway, who helped me structure the book. You made the book more readable than I could have done. Thanks Siri for more than helping me with the book.

I also want to thank the two reviewers who made a helpful feedback, which resulted in a new conclusion.

I also want to thank Associate Professor Arnulf Hauan, Nord University, for useful discussions on systemic thinking and taking the long view on history. I have never met anyone who has read *and* understood what is being read better than Arnulf. Thanks Arnulf for our discussions on Skype every week.

I would also like to thank Professor (full) Erik Steenfeldt Reinert ved Tallinn University of Technology. He used his time to read and comment upon some of my thoughts. He also showed me that Carlota Perez worked with some of the same problems as I did. This gave me knowledge I would not have got, if it had not been for Reinert. Thanks Reinert, you made my research more valuable, anyhow for myself, and it is my hope for someone else.

I also thank my nearest leader at Kristiania University College, Associate Professor Helene Sætersdal, and the President of Kristiania University College, Professor Trond Blindheim and Managing Director Solfrid Lind, who let me use my time researching this topic.

I also thank the librarian Live Vikøren at Kristiania University College for helping me when I needed it.

Last but not least, I want to thank the editors at Palgrave, especially Rachel Sangster and Tamsine O'Riordan.

Contents

List of Figures

1

Introduction

The following hypothesis is exemplified and examined in this book:

Hypothesis: Economic and institutional innovations lead to economic crises.

Implication: If the hypothesis is correct, then innovations, although they may be necessary for the dynamics of an economy, result in social consequences for individuals, organisations and society. The time-lag between economic and institutional innovations and economic crises is however difficult to gauge.

Contribution of the book: The same innovations that lead to the economic crisis, transform the economy and result in economic growth.

Main concepts: Three overarching concepts are used as a backdrop in the book: Threshold value, time-lag and feedback.

We exemplify the hypothesis and the contribution of the book in six economic crises through history, starting with the end of the Roman empire, through the tullips crises and the enduring financial crises from 2007.

Chapter 2 examines the assumption that there is a relationship between innovations and economic crises, with a particular focus on the economic crisis of the third century. The following question is examined: *Is there a*

© The Author(s) 2017
J.-A. Johannessen, *Innovations Lead to Economic Crises*,
DOI 10.1007/978-3-319-41793-6_1

relationship between innovations and the economic crises of the third century? The purpose of the chapter is to find out which innovations triggered the social mechanisms that led to the economic crisis of the third century.

The findings that emerge are that the following innovations fed through social mechanisms led to the crisis: New monetary policy (economic-financial innovation) and new leaders, institutions and power constellations occupy old positions (institutional and political innovations).

Chapter 3 examines the assumption that there is a relationship between innovations and economic crises, with a particular focus on the Amsterdam Tulip Crisis of 1637. The following question is examined: *Is there a relationship between innovations and economic crises?* The purpose of the chapter is to determine which innovations triggered the social mechanisms that led to the Tulip Crisis.

The findings that emerge are that the following innovations fed through social mechanisms led to the crisis: The establishment of the first limited liability company and the world's first stock exchange in 1602 (both institutional and political innovations); the Dutch East India Company (Dutch: Vereenigde Oost-Indische Compagnie), VOC, "United East India Company"), which was granted the authority to use military force in the name of the state (an institutional, political innovation); tulip bulbs were introduced into the market (a financial, product innovation); "*Windhandel*" ("Wind Trade"), i.e. the first "futures" market (an economic and financial product innovation); and the breakthrough of mercantile economics in Europe (an institutional, cultural innovation).

Chapter 4 examines the assumption that there is a relationship between innovations and economic crises, with a special focus on the economic crisis in Britain in 1720. The Mississippi Bubble and the economic crisis in France are described and analysed as well, because the British and French economic crises were interwoven. The following question is considered: *Is there a relationship between innovations and economic crises?* The purpose of the investigation is to discover which innovations triggered the social mechanisms that led to the economic crisis of 1720.

The findings presented reveal that the following innovations, working through social mechanisms, brought about the crisis: the establishment of the London Stock Exchange in 1698 (institutional, political innovation); new public–private loan schemes (institutional, political innovation); the English Revolution in 1688, and the Peace of Utrecht in 1713 (institutional, political innovations); the Mercantilist doctrine dominated European economic thinking (institutional, cultural innovation); and the emergence of options, lotteries, "futures" and new paper money (economic and financial product innovations).

Chapter 5 examines the assumption that there is a relationship between innovations and economic crises, with a particular focus on the economic crisis that began in 1873 and continued until 1879 in the US, and until 1893 in Europe. The following question is examined: *Is there a relationship between innovations and the economic crisis of 1873–1893?* The purpose of the chapter is to determine which innovations triggered the social mechanisms that led to the economic crisis in 1873.

The findings that emerge are that the following innovations fed through social mechanisms that led to the crisis: Railway construction (economic, technological innovation); new credit facilities (economic and financial product innovations); the electric telegraph (economic product innovation); the steam engine (economic product innovation); the unification of Germany (institutional, political innovation); and free trade, a political idea that emerged as the dominant economic model in the 1850s and 1860s (institutional, cultural innovation).

Chapter 6 examines the assumption that there is a relationship between innovations and economic crises, with a special focus on the economic crisis in the 1930s. The following question will be considered: *Is there a relationship between innovations and the economic crisis of the 1930s?* The purpose of the investigation is to discover which innovations triggered the social mechanisms that led to the economic crisis of the 1930s.

The findings presented reveal that the following innovations, working through social mechanisms, brought about the crisis of the 1930s: The founding of the Soviet Union (institutional, political innovation). Electrification; the combustion engine; the Bessemer Converter in steel production; the steam turbine; the light bulb; the discovery of electromagnetic waves; the radio; the telephone; ammonia synthesis; aspirin; assembly lines; the electric motor in vehicles (amongst other devices); electrification of trains; diesel engines (1893); the first aircraft; tractors, etc. (all economic, technological product innovations). The zeitgeist's ethos: Get rich quick without working hard (institutional, cultural innovation).

Chapter 7 examines the assumption that there is a relationship between innovations and economic crises. The specific analysis will focus on the ongoing economic crisis that started in the autumn of 2007. The following question is considered: *Is there a relationship between innovations and the economic crisis that was triggered in 2007?* The purpose of the investigation is to discover which innovations triggered the social mechanisms that led to the economic crisis.

The findings presented reveal that the following innovations, working through social mechanisms, brought about the crisis: globalisation (institutional, political innovation), modular flexibility (economic, organisational innovation), internet and personal computers (economic, technological innovation), the dollar standard and a credit-driven economy, as well as several financial product-innovations (economic and financial innovations), and the ethos of the age: What's in it for me? (institutional, cultural innovation).

Chapter 8 Conclusion, discusses innovation policy, or what to do with the knowledge that innovation leads to economic crises. Chapter 8 answer the question readers may have when read the book: So what? The answer is framed as a policy-model, which can be used by management and political leadership.

The Theoretical Basis for the Relationship Between Innovations and Economic Crises

Neal[1] and Paul[2] indicate relationships between financial innovations and the South Sea Bubble, but only to some extent. Reinhart and Rogoff also give some indication of a relationship between innovations and economic

---

[1] Neal (1990: 90).

[2] Paul (2011: 101; 116–117). Paul perhaps comes closest to making a link between innovation and economic crises. She has expressed the following in her conclusion on the South Sea Bubble: "The presence of naive investors during periods of innovation seems to be important in several well-known episodes, Tulipmania, the Mississippi Bubble, the Dotcom boom and others have attracted untried investors into the markets." (Paul 2011: 116–117). This is, however, the only thing Paul says about this relationship. It is notable that Paul suggests that it is the "untried investor" that cause crises. If experience could prevent crises, then Paul implies that the market is not a rational institution, but in the hands of inexperienced people who can lead the world into one crisis after

crises.[3] The clearest evidence of a relationship is given in Schumpeter's concept of "creative destruction". However, Schumpeter does not explore the relationship between innovations and economic crises. In general, he focuses on how new economic development arises out of the destruction of the old order.[4]

Schumpeter takes the concept of "creative destruction" from Karl Marx.[5] The first person to discuss the concept after Marx was the sociologist Werner Sombart. He describes "creative destruction" in the following way: "Wiederum, aber steigt aus der Zerstörung neuer schöpferisher Geist empor" ("*And again, from destruction rises a new creative spirit*").[6] It is reasonable to interpret Sombart as saying that it is the actual crisis that transforms the economy. If this is a correct interpretation, then Sombart, like Schumpeter, is concerned about what happens during a crisis. Sombart's point is that the new creative spirit rises up from the destruction. This is also the interpretation of Schumpeter's expression "creative destruction" that is argued for here.

Other social scientists who have used the original idea of creative destruction or "annihilation" used by Marx include Harvey,[7] Berman[8] and Castells.[9] Moreover, Mensch[10] is also of the opinion that innovations occur in clusters in the depression phase of a long economic wave. Van Duijn points to the time lag between an invention (discovery) and innovation, when there is a breakthrough in the market. This time lag can be as much as 40–50 years, as illustrated by the combustion engine.[11]

---

another. It is of course original to point out that a lack of experience is the cause of economic crises, but how appropriate this is is debatable.
[3] Reinhart & Rogoff (2009: 217, 141–174).
[4] Schumpeter (2010: 71–76).
[5] The term Marx and Engels use is "Annihilation". Marx & Engels (2002: 226); Marx (1993/1857: 750); Marx (1969/1863: 495–496).
[6] Sombart (1913: 207).
[7] Harvey (2007: 200–203).
[8] Berman (1988).
[9] Castells (2000).
[10] Mensch (1979).
[11] Van Duijn (1983).

This book is inspired by the ideas of Neo-Schumpeterian economics, as represented by economists such as Antonelli,[12] Peres[13] and Freeman[14]. Neo-Schumpeterians assume that: "crises along with innovation and structural change, [are] a constituent component of the ordinary functioning of the economic system." [15] However, the Neo–Schumpeterians, as far as I know, have not empirically examined the relationship between innovations, social mechanisms and economic crises throughout history.

Florida writes that when a crisis unfolds, the innovative process does not cease; on the contrary: "Innovation does not slow down during crises, but because the economy is depressed, they tend to accumulate and bunch up. They then come bursting forward as the economy recovers."[16] The same idea is found in Freeman,[17] Mensch[18] and the Nobel Prize winner in economics, Edmund Phelps.[19] The idea is that a crisis will spur inventions and innovations, which smooth the way out of the crisis. What is interesting here is that Schumpeter's concept of creative destruction, and the ideas of Florida, Freeman, Mensch and Phelps, examine how innovations can transform an economy during a crisis. This book examines how innovations *lead* to crises.

For the reasons stated above, it is important to distinguish between historical developments before, during and after an economic crisis, in order to bring out the difference between my assumption that innovations lead to economic crises and Schumpeter's concept of creative destruction, as well as Florida's, Freeman's and Mensch's ideas. My assumption throughout this book is that innovations provide a causal explanation of a given crisis.

If we examine research related to the long waves in an economy, called "Kondratiev Waves", then it may be possible that there is a connection

[12] Antonelli (1997, 2001).
[13] Peres (2002).
[14] Freeman (1997, 2008).
[15] Archibugi and Filippetti (2012: 18).
[16] Florida (2010: 12).
[17] Freeman (1997).
[18] Mensch (1983).
[19] Edmund Phelps, cited in Florida, (2010: 12, 191), note 7.

between my assumption that innovations lead up to crises and Mandel's[20] empirical substantiation that profit rates are above average in a long, expanding wave. Mandel relates these high profits to "scientific discoveries, technological innovation and technological diffusion." [21] However, he appears to have a narrow interpretation of innovation, applying it only to technological innovations.[22] In this book, technological innovations are only one part of the innovation concept. Regardless of the difference in the application of the concept of innovation, it seems as if Mandel's understanding of the long-wave expansion approaches my assumption that innovations cause economic crises. But while Mandel points to the development of the relative profit and above average profits as being the cause of the crises, I refer to innovation as being an important cause of economic crises. Nonetheless, one may argue that profit and innovation are only two sides of the same coin, economic development. To recap, in this book I use a broader concept and model of innovation than Mandel's concept of "innovation" as being limited to "technological innovations". Mandel[23] writes that it is not innovation in itself that brings the economy out of the crisis, but rather that profit is the main driving force. However, in reality it appears that sometimes profits drive innovation forward, while at other times factors far-removed from profit drive innovation,[24] suggesting that Mandel's ideas are not necessarily correct in every context.

Schumpeter's concept of creative destruction[25] is used in this book to explain how the economy recovers during a crisis —the old economy is destroyed and replaced by a new one based on innovations which lead the way out of the crisis. It has been shown, for instance, by, amongst others, Mensch,[26] Van Duijn[27] and Dosi[28] that technological innovations come

---

[20] Mandel (1995: 110).

[21] Mandel (1995: 110).

[22] Mandel (1995: 28–49).

[23] Mandel (1995: 113).

[24] Government initiated innovations had a major impact in Norway after the war, where the government initiated innovations in the fishing industry (refrigeration). This was not profitable, but was motivated by other factors (Johannessen 1980).

[25] Schumpeter (2010: 139).

[26] Mensch (1979).

[27] Van Duijn (1983).

[28] Dosi (2000).

in clusters, or figuratively, that they build up like flood water before it bursts through the dam walls at the end of a long downward wave. This, these authors argue, is what brings the economy out of a long slump. This can be understood through two processes. The first is described as creative destruction. The second process is the diffusion of innovations and the rapidity of this diffusion. An important point in an economic crisis, however, is that innovations work and spread slowly. It is here that one can imagine that creative destruction works to prepare the economy for the diffusion process, as Mensch has attempted to show.[29] It seems as if the forces that promote innovation are stronger than those that inhibit innovation during a crisis.[30] It appears, however, that a threshold value must be exceeded before diffusion processes can achieve the necessary speed.

This book proposes that the same innovations that lead to the crisis, facilitate the conditions during the crisis for the development of creative and new market initiatives, and lead the economy into growth after the crisis. If this assumption is correct it provides both theoretical and practical implications for economic and social behaviour.

---

[29] Mensch (1983, Chap. 4).
[30] Tinbergen and Kleinknecht (1987: 23–24).

2

The Long Economic Crisis of the Third Century

Introduction

The crisis of the third century is the first documented example where inflation became a problem in Europe[1] This can be seen by studying the metal content of contemporary coinage, and various imperial documents, for instance, ED,[2] which attempted to fix prices in the various parts of the Roman Empire.

The crisis of the third century lasted for more than 100 years, starting in AD 193 with Emperor Septimus Severus and ending in AD 337 with the death of Constantine the Great; consequently the third century is called the "long" century.[3]

The crisis of the third century also resulted in the first so-called economic "bubble" that we have records of. The bubble may be understood in terms of the devaluation of the coinage and the rise in prices of necessities. To exemplify this we can look at the price of wheat: in the first and

---

[1] Corbier (2005: 425).
[2] ED: The Edict of Diocletian (AD 303).
[3] Corbier (2005: 394).

© The Author(s) 2017
J.-A. Johannessen, *Innovations Lead to Economic Crises*,
DOI 10.1007/978-3-319-41793-6_2

second centuries the price of wheat from Egypt remained relatively stable at around 7–8 drachmas. However, this rose to 17–18 drachmas in the third century. It seems reasonable to assume that this rise in prices had significant social consequences for those people who were dependent on wheat imports. In addition, the silver content of the denarius fell from 85% to 5%,[4] resulting in hyperinflation, further reinforcing the negative trend.

In addition to economic problems and external enemies, there were also internal conflicts between the various power factions within the Roman Empire, as when several leaders proclaimed themselves emperor. The empire needed money, food, weapons and equipment for its army. Under such conditions it was difficult if not impossible to maintain an effective administration; consequently, a militaristic bureaucracy developed which assumed the responsibilities of the civil administration.

The social consequences of these changes mostly affected the lower classes, and there were several popular rebellions that were brutally crushed by military units.[5]

External pressure, internal civil war, urban population decline in the cities and general chaos, all led to a decline in production. Decline in agricultural production and outbreaks of disease, such as malaria, further reinforced the economic downturn in the third century.

Agricultural production declined, amongst other things, because dykes and canals were neglected; famine became a part of everyday existence for many under these circumstances. Survival came to be largely synonymous with self-sufficiency, and increased self-sufficiency meant a further decrease in trade, intensifying the economic downturn. In this situation, the authorities had to resort to force and repression to keep the wheels of the economy turning.[6]

Invasions, civil war, plagues and increased taxes led to several of the provinces breaking free of the empire and forming separate states. Multiple emperors ruled in the different parts of the empire during the civil wars, resulting in increased administrative costs. For instance, the

---

[4] Percival (1976: 43).
[5] Rostovtzeff (1998: 472).
[6] Frank (2005: 477–511).

establishment of several capitals with their own administrations led to increased costs, which all had to be covered by taxation. Another source of income was to increase the amount of coinage in circulation, thereby reducing the value of the currency.

Emperor Aurelian (AD 270–275) re-unified the empire. However, it was the reforms of the soldier–emperor Diocletian (AD 284–305) which re-established the unity of the Roman Empire. He appointed three co-emperors, or a "Tetrarchy",[7] under which Constantine was given control in the East and Licinius in the West. Constantine was the father of the later Constantine the Great; it was under Constantine the Great that the civil wars ceased, after his victory against co-emperor Maxentius in AD 312 and finally over co-emperor Licinius in AD 324.[8]

The chapter is organised as follows: First, an account of the background of the crisis is given. Second, the development of the crisis and some of the consequences are reviewed. Third, some of the relevant innovations and the social mechanisms which these triggered are examined. In conclusion, a model is developed, illustrating the relationship between innovation, social mechanisms and the economic crisis of the third century.

Background

The population of Rome during the time of Emperor Augustus (27 BC–14 AD) is estimated to have been approximately one million; of these, approximately 200,000 were slaves.[9] It is estimated that approximately 320,000 in Rome had access to free grain during Augustus' reign (Rickman 1980:10–11). The amount of grain needed to feed such a large population was huge, estimated to be roughly 90 kg per capita per annum, and had to be imported from the provinces (Rickman 1980:10).

There was a great decrease in the population during the reign of Emperor Marcus Aurelius (AD 161–180), which meant there was also a reduction in the demand for grain. It is estimated that 25 % of the popu-

---

[7] "Tetrarchy" means "the leadership of four people".
[8] Corbier (2005: 393).
[9] Rickman (1980: 10)

lation died during the plague. The plague and the economic downturn resulted in a decrease in the population to roughly 500,000 in Rome (AD 273).[10] The decrease from one million people to 500,000 indicates not only an economic crisis but also a social and cultural crisis. This part is organised as follows. First we look at economic factors. Then we will consider new attitudes towards trade and markets. Finally, we examine the political factors.

Economic Factors

The local, city tax was collected in various ways. Much of it was collected at the point of consumption, not unlike today's sales tax, for example in the form of ferry fees, customs duties for goods in and out of the cities, fees for those who sold goods in the market, water charges, admissions fees to public baths, fines, etc.[11] The cities could not impose new taxes or change old taxes without first informing the emperor.

Corbier[12] writes that the debt burden was a major problem at all social levels in the third century. The interest rate on loans was 1 % per month. Having a large loan could have serious consequences, to the extent that people could be forced to sell everything they owned, including their children into slavery, if they were unable to pay back what they owed plus interest.[13]

Mining and the stone industry provided important products, such as different types of tools, coinage, roads and buildings. In the second century, the mining industry was especially important for the production of jewellery; the most important mines were owned by the emperor,[14] and all the metal mines in the second century were controlled by imperial procurators. There were three types of workers in mines: free workers who were paid for their work, slaves and convicts.[15] The free workers

---

[10] http://en.wikipedia.org/wiki/History_of_Rome
[11] Corbier (2005: 388).
[12] Corbier (2005: 427).
[13] Corbier (2005: 427).
[14] Corbier (2005: 406).
[15] Corbier (2005: 407).

received a wage that was equal to the wages of a soldier in the Roman army.[16] The mines were located in the provinces, such as Hispania, Gaul and to some extent in the province of Tuscany; from Egypt to Armenia; and up to the Empire's northern border.

New Attitudes Towards Trade and Markets

There were two main categories of business people in the Roman Empire: moneylenders and traders. The moneylenders were in principal bankers because they lent money against payment (interest), thus enabling trade. The moneylenders also sold goods in bulk, not unlike today's wholesalers. Traders were mostly plebeians and freed slaves. Traders also ran stables for posting horse exchange and sold their goods from shops along the Roman roads. They were also present at the front during military campaigns, where they sold a variety of goods to soldiers.

However, the trading market was of so little importance that the administrative system that ensured the supply of food supply to Rome completely bypassed it.[17] In other words, as Erdkamp argues, it was poor market channels that necessitated intervention from the government to ensure the food supply to the cities of the Roman Empire.

Of interest to our discussion are contemporary attitudes towards trade, and the question of which social groups participated in trade in the Roman Empire. We know, for example, that in the Republic and early Empire, senators were prohibited by law from engaging in maritime trade.[18] Trade was not regarded as a worthy profession for senators. In spite of this, it was through involvement in trade that some people became part of the upper social strata of the Roman Empire.

Nevertheless, senators managed through intermediaries such as freed slaves, friends and the aristocracy in the cities to acquire some of the profits from the lucrative trade within the Roman Empire, and between the Roman Empire and the Far East (i.e. India and China). Thus, there seems to have been a two-fold approach to trade, one expressed in law and

---

[16] Cuvigny (1996: 139–145).

[17] Erdkamp (2005: 6).

[18] DÁrms (1981).

one applied in practice; this was thus a distinction between attitudes and action. Attitudes could be enshrined in law, literature on the matter, senators' speeches and written documents, and in other ways. The actions, however, are the specific practices that were carried out in everyday life.

Most cities lived off the revenue that landowners and the government obtained from rural areas, such as production from the mines, agricultural production, taxes and duties, etc. This revenue from rural areas was concentrated and used in cities.[19] In this way, the cities provide an indicator of the economic condition of the Roman Empire.

The wealthy built monumental houses in the cities. These monuments and their statues also provide evidence of the period of greatness of the cities at both ends of the economic crisis in the Roman Empire; the first period coincides with the beginning of the decline, while the last period of urban development coincides with the end of the economic crisis.

The markets in the cities were largely dominated by the plebeians, the middle class and the lower middle class, as well as freed slaves. This reflects clearly the attitudes towards trade mentioned above. However, these traders could become very rich through their trading activities.[20]

The markets in the Roman Empire were mainly located in the cities. As cities grew and their populations exceeded a certain level, the surrounding rural areas were unable to supply the urban population of a city with their needs. As this threshold was exceeded, the city's needs triggered trade in ever-larger areas. The burgeoning population of the cities thus had a locomotive effect on trade in the Roman Empire. It is reasonable to assume that the cities and the emperor's demands for goods and services are the two main driving factors of the Roman economy.

Political Factors

In the second century AD it was more the rule than the exception that the reigning emperors adopted individuals who possessed certain qualities

---

[19] Corbier (2005: 408).

[20] The Emperor Nero (AD 54–68) was born a plebeian, since his father belonged to this social stratum. Although Nero does not belong to the period we are examining here, it may be interesting to know that he invested considerably in trade and used trade as a diplomatic tool, even if this is not what he is most well known for.

and abilities, and that these in turn succeeded as the new emperor,[21] who would then be approved by the Senate. Some examples illustrate this practice in the second century: Emperor Trajan (AD 98–117) was adopted by Nerva (AD 96–98); Trajan adopted Hadrian (AD 117–138); Hadrian adopted Antonius (AD 138–161) and Antonius adopted two sons, Lucius Verus (AD 161–169) and Marcus Aurelius, who ruled together.

However, an institutional innovation was introduced by Marcus Aurelius when he broke with the above tradition by making his own son Commodus his successor (AD 180–192). However, Commodus was a man ill-equipped to be emperor.[22] We need to go back in history 100 years to Titus, who succeeded his father Vespasian in AD 79, to find an instance of the father–son relationship with regard to imperial succession. When Commodus was assassinated in AD 192, the Praetorian Guard began to sell the imperial office to the highest bidder (in the sense of someone who could provide them with the best power and position within the Empire).[23] This led to soldiers on various fronts[24] nominating their own generals as emperors; thus, it was often the generals who promised the best conditions for their soldiers who were nominated as emperors by their armies. In this sense, it may be said that the weak imperial succession institution contributed to laying the foundation for the crisis of the third century. On the death of Commodus, there were several claimants to the title of Roman emperor; Septimus Severus (AD 193–211), the nominee of, finally emerged victorious. On his deathbed he advised his sons to enrich the soldiers, and scorn the rest of the population.[25] Of course we don't know with certainty if this deathbed speech is true or not, but it characterises the zeitgeist of the times that followed. Emperor Caracalla (AD 198–217), the eldest son of Septimius Severus instituted a rule of tyranny in the Roman Empire, beginning with the murder of his own brother in AD 211 and followed by massacres and persecutions throughout the whole of the empire.

---

[21] Luttwalk (1979: 127).

[22] Luttwalk (1979: 127).

[23] Luttwalk (1979: 128).

[24] This concerned three fronts: Britannia, Danube and the Eastern front (Euphrates, Syria or Egypt)

[25] Watson (1999: 5).

The civil wars made it easier for external enemies on the borders in the north and east to penetrate the empire for plunder and conquest. The northern part of Gaul (present day France), the Balkans and Syria were completely destroyed as a result, at least when viewed from a Roman perspective.[26] It was in the third century that the Goths began to move westward from southern Russia, and also during this period that the Franks (Germanic tribes) occupied land in the Rhine region; for example, Caracalla had to fight the German tribes who invaded in AD 213 on the Raetic front in the north (present day Switzerland). The pressure only increased from the northern front, and two years later the whole of the Rhine front had to be defended against invading tribes. By the middle of the third century, the invading tribes had occupied the whole of Gaul and parts of northern Hispania. The invaders had also penetrated the mountain passes of northern Italia.[27] The Goths also attacked on the Danube front, as well as invading the Black Sea with their fleet, attacking Asia Minor and Greece several times in the third century.[28] It was also during this period that the Persians invaded the Roman Empire from the east.

The Development of the Crisis

This part is organised as follows. We first consider the economic factors, then briefly describe the emergence of new attitudes towards trade. Rome's port Ostia is used to exemplify the development of the crisis. Finally, we examine the political factors.

Economic Factors

Civil war, wars against external enemies, payments to the army, administration and rewards to those who supported Septimus Severus, led to the devaluation of the currency. In practice, this meant that more money was

---

[26] Frank (2005: 484).

[27] Frank (2005: 486).

[28] Frank (2005: 486), mentions several attacks by the Goths on Greece in the years AD 256, 258, 263, 264, 265, 267, and often in the years between AD 270 to 284.

injected into the Roman economy. This was accomplished by reducing the silver content of the coins and using cheaper metals, such as bronze and copper, to replace the silver. The silver coin denarius[29] was by the middle of the third century only a debased version of the coin that had been in use for more than 300 years.

Septimus Severus completely reformed the monetary system, something that may be understood as a monetary policy innovation. The de facto devaluation that had existed in the previous 20–30 years was now an official devaluation.[30] Throughout the third century each new emperor—including Caracalla, Aurelian, Diocletian and Constantine— introduced new monetary standards in order to gain control of the economy, which had gone completely out of control as a result of Severus' new monetary policies. We do not know exactly what happened, but the following factors seem to have played a role, alone or in combination. New currency units were minted, and the number of coins in circulation increased. The authority to mint new coins was given to more people and institutions. When Severus waged war against Mesopotamia he needed money. He produced more coins and allowed more money to be minted in the east of the empire.[31] The same thing happened when Emperor Caracalla led a campaign against Parthia (present day Iran).

The importance of minting new coins is illustrated in the following account. In AD 238, there were two mints producing coins for the Roman Empire, located in Rome and Antioch. These mints also included a total of nine workshops that were part of the production process of the various coins. By AD 270, the number of mints had increased from two to seven, and by this time there were 33 workshops included in the production process.[32] There are several factors that indicate that the flow of money in circulation increased significantly from the middle of the

---

[29] One pound of gold (ca. 453 grams) in AD 301 cost ca. 72,000 denarii. The relationship between gold and silver was approximately 1:12, since a pound of silver cost 6000 denarii (see Reynolds 1995: 22). Gold coins were called Solidus (the Latin word for 'solid').

[30] Corbier, 2005:344.

[31] Corbier (2005: 344).

[32] Corbier (2005: 345).

third century,[33] while by the start of the fourth century, there is much evidence to suggest that the money supply had decreased.[34]

The "Antonianius" coin, which is thought to have been worth two denarii, was introduced by Caracalla in AD 215. It was first produced as a silver coin, but was quickly debased with bronze. Buyers and sellers in the market quickly realised that the coin had fallen in value, and adjusted prices of goods accordingly, increasing inflation. Large quantities of this coin were produced, and after a period of time only bronze was used in its production. By the end of the third century, the Roman Empire was beset by hyperinflation.

The Roman gold coin, which had been minted from pure gold up until the middle of the third century, was debased under Emperor Valerian (AD 253–260) and Emperor Gallienus (AD 253–268), which we know from "The Edict of Diocletian". There were some periods during the third century when inflation was very high, whereas at other times it was more under control.[35] The period AD 253–270 seems to have been a time of high inflation, if inflation is understood in terms of the reduction in the content of precious metal in the Roman coins.

Although the coins were minted in several places, and Egypt had its own currency, the emperor had a monopoly on the minting of coins. Monetary policy was thus controlled by the emperor. From the middle of the third century the minting of coins became highly decentralised. Emperor Valerius (AD 253–260), and his son Gallienus (emperor AD 260–268), introduced the minting of coins close to where the armies were stationed, perhaps in an attempt to forestall the political and military riots which occurred if a particular area had a shortage of coins, and this led to political and military riots.[36]

In AD 259, the minting of coins in Gaul was the responsibility of the first Gallic Emperor, Postumus (AD 260–269); the Gallic Empire lasted from AD 260–274. It had two mints, in Trier and Cologne, where coins were produced.

---

[33] Corbier (2005: 345–346).
[34] Callu (1980: 175–254); King (1980: 152).
[35] Corbier (2005: 338).
[36] Corbier (2005: 351).

The British part of the Roman Empire was ruled by Emperor Carausius (AD 286–293) who was assassinated by his finance minister Allectus (who became emperor in AD 293–296); it had its own mints, the most important of which was located in London.

The troops' wages also provide an indication of the price developments in the third century. Under Emperor Caracalla soldiers were paid 600 denarii a year.[37] However, by the end of the third century this had been increased to 3300 denarii, and in some cases as much as 8000 to 12,000 denarii.[38]

Another indication of the price and cost developments in the third century can be found in the "The Edict of Diocletian". In his edict, Diocletian attempted to prevent inflation by price controls, suggesting that inflation in the third century must have been perceived as a problem by the authorities. Although inflation control was not successful, it illustrates that Diocletian attempted to come to grips with development in prices and costs, and that this was a challenge the authorities took seriously. It was first during Constantine the Great's reign that inflation was stabilised, through a monetary policy reform in AD 310.

One of the innovations of the period under review was the establishment of state businesses and workshops, which occurred during the Tetrarchy (AD 293–313). It seems reasonable to view this as a type of government intervention in the market during this period. It is possible that these national workshops and businesses were established to ensure the supply of goods to the army and other state institutions, at a time when the empire's economy was in a state of crisis.

There is a well-preserved Roman document, called the "Notitia Dignitatum", which describes the various contemporary state institutions.[39] There were 35 public workshops[40] established and spread throughout the Roman Empire during the Tetrarchy. These workshops

---

[37] Under special circumstances wages were increased, such as during campaigns and war expeditions, etc.
[38] Corbier (2005: 382).
[39] Fairlay (2009).
[40] Silvius (2010).

included spinning mills and weapons factories (although state-owned weapons factories had existed before this time as well).[41]

The tendency towards the disintegration of the Roman Empire in the mid-third century—Gaul seceded in 260–274 AD, and Britannia in 287–296 AD.[42]

However, this did not result in reduced yields from the mines because the rebels needed both silver and gold for their coins and metal for their weapons.

On the basis of the above description, it is difficult to claim that the mining industry was particularly affected by the crisis of the third century. We know that both famine and epidemics also affected the mining industry, but this sector was not alone in that regard. The development of the mining industry may be viewed as resulting from three factors[43]:

1. Demand from Rome decreased due to civil wars.
2. Military leaders at the front line needed metal for weapons.
3. Local rebels took control of the mines.

New Attitudes Towards Trade

A change occurred amongst the Roman elite in the third century. The class that ranked just below the patricians, called the knight class, assumed a new position within the power hierarchy. These were people, often from the provinces, especially from the Balkans, who rose through the ranks of the military; this class was also involved in trading. The best example of this is Emperor Diocletian, who was from a low-status family in Dalmatia in the Balkans. After advancing through the ranks of the military, he ended up as emperor. Under Diocletian, the military leaders were drawn to a greater extent from the provinces, at the expense of the Roman aristocracy. The civil administration of the empire also came from the provinces to an increasing extent. This may explain why attitudes towards engaging in trade shifted during the course of the third century:

---

[41] Coulston (1988).
[42] Birley (1992), chap. XIV.
[43] Corbier (2005: 407).

it came to be considered as a more acceptable activity for the people of higher social classes to participate in.

Rome's Port Ostia as an Example of the Development of the Crisis

The fate of the port city of Rome, Ostia, embodies the crisis in the third century. The emperors had created the demand for buildings, roads, expansion of the port area, various defence constructions and canals in Ostia. With the devolution of central government, internal conflicts and economic hard times, the port of Ostia went into decline. As a result of the lack of demand for new buildings, the brick industry was also greatly reduced.

The brick industry demanded both management and craft skills. When the demand for bricks declined, the industry was reduced to being produced by individual craftsmen. This development is evident because the bricks were stamped with marks. In other words, each brick had its own "mark", so it was possible to know where it originated from. This functioned both as a quality mark and "branding" for those who produced the bricks. For the buyer of the brick, the mark could also act as an "insurance policy" in relation to who was responsible, if the brick did not meet certain quality standards.

Another indication of Ostia's decline is how it was governed. Until the third century, Ostia had its own city government, council and magistrate. But during the course of the third century, the city was put under the direct command of the emperor in Rome, who appointed a local procurator who ruled in his name.

Ostia and other cities grew due to the large volume of trade (and profits from it). However, when Rome imported less from overseas in the third century, trade and profits declined, contributing to a decline in population.[44]

Plague, which ravaged the empire throughout the third century, also contributed to a decline in the population. The cities were first hit by the

---

[44] Meiggs (1997: 85).

"Antonine" plague, which lasted from 165 AD to 180, and then by the "Plague of Cyprian", which lasted from 251–270 AD. The plagues and changes in trading patterns led to a drop in the demand for grain, wine and oil, further exacerbating Ostia's decline. In addition to this, the third century was troubled by the civil wars between competing emperors.

The largest buildings in Ostia were often built because emperors wanted something to symbolise their power and greatness. But when they had more than enough to occupy their time in struggling to retain power in the third century, the demand for large new building projects decreased sharply. Construction and dock workers lost their jobs, retail sales declined and other workers were affected by the general economic downturn and lost their jobs.

Throughout the second century, power over the independent city-states of the empire had been centralised.[45] Ostia and Porthus had a special position in this administrative innovation, because they constituted the lifeblood of Rome.

The inhabitants of Ostia and Porthus lived off agriculture, fisheries, crafts and trade. Agriculture and fisheries provided stabilised living conditions for their citizens, when trade dwindled in the third century. Fishing grounds were to be found both on the Tiber and along the coast of Ostia and Porthus.[46]

During Ostia's heydays, shipbuilding probably constituted the main craft industry; another important craft industry was the production of lamps. It seems to be the case that the rich and poor bought different types of lamps; the poor used lamps made of baked clay, while the wealthy used lamps which were imported from Athens, Etruria and southern Italia, and later from Rome's colonies in Africa. Black glazed lamps seem to have been in vogue in the third and fourth century for the wealthier classes.[47]

In addition to boat-building and lamp production in Ostia, there were also shoemakers and tool makers, who were involved, amongst other things, in the production of jewellery and fine metalwork; this is evident from the inscriptions on tombstones. The craft industry was carried out

---

[45] Meiggs (1997: 85).
[46] Meiggs (1997: 266–268).
[47] Meiggs (1997: 270–271).

largely in the houses where the craftsmen lived; some rooms in the dwellings were reserved for this production.[48] Of course, the craft industry in ancient Ostia is clearly different from large-scale industrial production in industrial societies. However, there was also large-scale production in Ostia (in addition to the brick industry), such as the bakeries. One of the bakeries we know occupied about 9900 square metres, and another was even larger. This large-scale production was probably delivered to local outlets.[49] However, when demand for bread declined in the third century due to the decline in population, it is reasonable to assume that this large-scale production was particularly hard-hit because the cost of production must be regarded as relatively high; smaller local bakeries could survive longer when based on the family member's "free" labour.

Outlets for the production of craftsmen and toolmakers were generally a large room facing the street. Behind this room was a room where some of the production took place. A staircase from this room and up to the first floor led to the area where the family lived.[50] A shopping street consisted of an accumulation of such businesses, where craft workers and their families lived.

The aqueducts that supplied water to public and private buildings were not mass produced but constructed by local craftsmen.[51] The demand for such constructions and the repairs of these diminished during the crisis of the third century, resulting in negative consequences for the craftsmen concerned.

Wine and oil were stored in large vats, which were immersed in the warehouse floor, keeping the temperature cool and stable. The trade in wine and oil in Ostia, and probably throughout the empire, was organised into craft guilds; this is evident from the study of tombstone inscriptions.[52]

---

[48] Meiggs (1997: 271).

[49] Meiggs (1997: 271).

[50] Meiggs (1997: 272).

[51] Local production processes are evident from the markings on the bricks used in the building industry. About half of the marks are those of imperial craftsmen, probably from Rome, while the rest are from local craftsmen in Ostia, cf. Meiggs 1997: 272.

[52] Meiggs (1997: 276–277).

Grain was stored in large buildings specially designed for the purpose. When demand fell in the third century, the grain warehouses and storage facilities for wine and oil became less important. One can imagine that the price of warehouse space sharply decreased. It is also reasonable to assume that houses and other buildings in Ostia fell dramatically in price during the third century because of the decline in demand and trade. It is thus conceivable that this led to the bursting of a price bubble in house prices in Ostia. This hypothesis is supported by the fact that several buildings were converted so that they served other functions than they had previously during the course of the Severan dynasty (AD 193–235).

Ostia and Porthus had three main functions in relation to Rome. First, they were ports for imported goods, which came from other provinces in Italia, such as wine from the east coast and oil and wine from the provinces around the Mediterranean. Second, the ports had warehouse facilities for goods that were needed in Rome; grain is an example of such a product. Third, these two ports functioned as centres where agreements with captains and ship-owners were entered into regarding tariffs and cargoes to and from Ostia and Porthus to the ports in the Mediterranean.

Political Factors

During the period of Emperor Caracalla, a vicious cycle developed in which the generals who were successful at driving back invading peoples along the borders were quickly proclaimed emperors by their soldiers. This resulted in the army in question competing with the current emperor in order to gain power over the empire as a whole. A small force would be garrisoned to defend the borders of the empire. However, the enemies along the borders often discovered this weakness and stormed the borders. If the commander who returned to defend the borders was successful in defeating the invading forces, then the soldiers could proclaim him emperor. In this way, the empire was both prone to internal civil wars and a relatively easy target for border invasions. The many commanders who were proclaimed emperor could more correctly be termed usurpers, and they were often quickly defeated. Few of them were approved by the in Rome. The Senate, however, declined noticeably in importance with regard to imperial power from the end of the second century onwards (Watson 1999: 5). One of the results of these political tensions was that the empire was difficult to control in the third century. This was one of the reasons why the idea of shared imperial power gained ground; another reason was to clarify the line of succession. The division of power led eventually to the Tetrarchy under Emperor Diocletian beginning in AD 293. This is also considered by historians as signalling the end of the crisis of the third century, and the restoration of the empire as a whole. The Tetrarchy lasted until AD 313, when Constantine became emperor in the West and Licinius in the East.

In AD 235, Alexander Severus (AD 222–235) was murdered by his soldiers. This event ushered in 50 years of civil war in the empire, which lasted until the assassination of Emperor Carinus (AD 282–285) in AD 285, when emperor Diocletian came to power. There were 24 more or less legitimate emperors of the Roman Empire between the reigns of Severus and Diocletian, and many more who were declared emperor by their troops. The legitimate emperors ruled on average for a period of about 3 years.[53]

During the 50-year-long civil war, the soldiers on the various fronts nominated their own generals as emperors; over sixty persons were declared emperors during this period, and almost all of these met their deaths by the sword.[54] It appears that the military ethos and the logic of victory were the primary basis for governing the empire in this 50-year period.

It is reasonable to assume that it was the double threat from both the northern front and the east that resulted in the empire giving way to the invasion forces. In the east the Persians under new leadership[55] had unified their whole kingdom, and could now pose a real threat to the Roman Empire. On the northern front, the enemies of Rome had also grown stronger through the formation of alliances and federations.

---

[53] Luttwalk (1979: 128).

[54] Watson (1993: 3).

[55] While the Persians were previously organised into semi-autonomous vassal states under a superior authority, under the Sassanids they were organised as a unified state (Lutwak 1979: 150).

Some Consequences of the Crisis

One of the consequences of the third century crisis was Diocletian's reforms: these centralised administration, divided the provinces into smaller units and introduced a more effective system of taxation.[56]

It is not until Constantine the Great's reign, and after he had defeated co-Emperor Licinius in AD 324, that a new monetary policy, or rather a currency system, was introduced in the empire. At the end of Constantine's reign, the centre for coin production moved to Constantinople, while other minting institutions were moved to other cities in the Eastern Roman Empire, including Sirmium on the Danube. Carthage, London and Ticinum ceased to produce coins.[57] In this way, Constantine took control of the economy by controlling monetary policy.

One can argue that the Roman Empire was a demand-driven economy, where demand was largely centred around imperial power. As this demand stalled or declined during the third century, this led to a negative spiral for all those who participated in production, distribution and trade. This downward spiral was rapidly reinforced, when people were left overnight without income, contributing to the decrease in demand for goods and services. To get such a centralised demand-driven economy back on its feet, it was necessary to re-establish central power, which occurred only after Constantine re-established control over the whole of the Roman Empire.

It is reasonable to assume, with Charlesworth, that the centralisation of the rights of ownership of land properties in the hands of the emperor and a few land owners was a major reason for the collapse in agricultural production during the crisis in the third century. The various emperors were unable to sustain demand and control of production, resulting in the decline of agriculture in many provinces. This may also be part of the explanation as to why it was relatively easy for the invaders to conquer the empire's northern provinces in the fifth century. It was only in AD 533 that Emperor Justinian I (AD 527–565) in the Eastern Roman Empire started the reconquest of the northern provinces from the German tribes.

---

[56] Jones (1986: 448–462).
[57] Corbier (2005: 349).

It appears that several of the Roman mining towns in Britannia in the second and third centuries were abandoned.[58] This suggests that the crisis of the third century had major consequences for the British mining industry, towns and trade; it also indicates that the crisis spread to many parts of the empire.

Faith in Roman currency was sharply reduced in the third century, when the Roman currency was devalued by reducing the content of gold and silver in coins, and when several competing emperors produced their own coins. This is illustrated by the dearth of archaeological discoveries of Roman third century coins in India. Based on archaeological findings, it is reasonable to say that trade between the Roman Empire and India was reduced for much of the third century, but picked up again in the fourth century.[59] This indicates that the economic crisis of the third century stretched all the way from Britannia in the west to the Indian subcontinent in the east.

During the crisis, "all cities were worse off", says Liebesschuetz.[60] It also appears that a network of cities evolved as a result of the crisis.[61] The tendency was for the provinces to become smaller administrative units, and for new cities to assume administrative functions in these new administrative provinces. This led to some provincial cities becoming increasingly important, while other cities became less important.

The decline in many though not all the cities in the western part of the empire during the third century[62] has left unresolved issues with regard to what really happened. The immediate explanation is that there was a substantial reduction in population in the cities. However, it appears that the different towns and cities had different development patterns. In towns and cities where trade and production played a major role, it seems reasonable to assume that the population was reduced as a result of reduced demand. In the areas where cities were more self-contained units, and less dependent on trade, it is conceivable that the crisis played

---

[58] Liddle (2002).
[59] Tomber (2008: 161).
[60] Liebesschuetz (1992: 9).
[61] Millett (1990: 143–151).
[62] Liebeschuetz (1992: 10)

a smaller role. This, for example, seems to be the case of towns and cities in northern Britannia, although they were dependent on the import of olives and wine.[63]

One of the results of the crisis of the third century was that some towns and cities, for example, in Britannia, experienced a decrease in population of approximately 50 % between AD 220 and into the fourth century.[64] One of the reasons that the population declined in London during the crisis may be that the city was a centre of trade in goods, including wine and olives. When these activities were reduced, unemployment resulted in the movement of people into rural areas in search of sustenance and employment.

Analysis

Institutional Innovations

The crisis of the long third century was triggered by a significant institutional innovation: new leaders, institutions and power constellations were able to occupy the old positions of power.

Another institutional innovation, which did not trigger the crisis, but certainly amplified it, was the new approach to trade, a new way of thinking if you will. This innovation may be said to constitute an institutional cultural innovation. The innovation involved trade becoming a legitimate activity for the Roman upper classes, which promoted trade at the expense of other institutions in the empire. I have chosen to include it in the description here although this innovation did not trigger the social mechanisms that caused the crisis; it is included because it can be assumed that it exacerbated the crisis, after it had been triggered. However, for pedagogical reasons, I have not included this innovation in figure 1 below.

---

[63] Millett (1990: 159–163).
[64] Reece (1992: 139).

New Leaders, Institutions and Power Constellations

This is an institutional policy innovation in the Roman Empire with very serious consequences, as described above. These institutional changes triggered internal stresses in the structures of power and contributed to civil war.

The break in the adoption convention regarding the nomination of new emperors was one such institutional innovation. This led to the sons of emperors inheriting the reign from their fathers; these rulers were not necessarily the best qualified, and they did not always possess the necessary skills for governing the empire. This led to a system of government which the leading power institutions, primarily the Praetorian Guard, did not always concur with. Consequently, the latter began to auction off the imperial office, leading to internal tensions and ultimately civil war. The result was that Septimus Severus and his successors came to power in the Roman Empire. This is also seen as the beginning of the crisis in the long third century. When the civil wars began in AD 238 and lasted for 50 years, this resulted in internal tensions so great that the defence of the borders was weakened, resulting in invasions on several fronts.

A New Attitude Towards Trade Undermines the Importance of Established Institutions

It seems reasonable to assume that this change in mindset led to the focus of the upper class turning away from the military system, and income from landed estates, towards profits that could be made from trade.

Trade and traders did not have a high social status in the Roman Empire before this change in mindset occurred. This is indicated amongst other things by the fact that senators were not allowed to participate in maritime trade. The attitude towards trade changed in the empire at the same time that new men came to power. These individuals had been involved in trade before they entered the upper strata of the empire. It can be assumed that this also changed attitudes towards trade. One can say that trading became a legitimate activity for the upper classes as the new rulers of the provinces gained positions in the power hierarchy.

Economic Innovations

A new monetary policy constituted a financial innovation in the Roman Empire that had special significance for the crisis of the third century. This monetary policy reduced the value of money, which eventually led to inflation and social conflicts.

The crisis of the third century triggered the first known financial bubble. Gold coins disappeared and silver coins were worth less. This was part of what happened under Emperor Caracalla. Later Emperor Claudius II (AD 268–270), and then Emperor Aurelian (AD 270–275), introduced new monetary units, which broke with the classical principle that the coins should contain a certain amount of silver or gold.[65] From now on, the monetary unit was based on "faith" in the currency because the empire as represented by the emperor guaranteed the value of the monetary units. This must be regarded as an innovation in the history of money, where faith in the currency, as opposed to the actual value of the silver or gold content, became the foundation of the currency's value.

One of the consequences of the price increases was financial speculation, especially related to trading in various types of goods.[66] An example of the consequences of such speculation is the city of Mylasa in the Caria region in south-western Anatolia, where the city council had to protect banks in the period around AD 209–211 because the city's supply was at stake.[67] There was wild speculation in which people trying to profit from the price bubble on various necessities. What happened was probably profit-making involving the exchange of silver and gold by the banks (moneylenders), who had a monopoly on lending activity in cities. When the currency units decreased in value, the value of gold and silver increased. In this way, those who had silver and gold gained tremendously in wealth. After a period of time, the banks (moneylenders) closed and refused to exchange coins into silver and gold. Banks closing in emergency situations seems thus to be a phenomenon that existed in

---

[65] This is analogous to the departure from the gold standard in recent times.

[66] Rostovtzeff (1998: 472).

[67] Rostovtzeff (1998: 472).

antiquity. The banks, however, were forced by local military leaders to re-open for the exchange of imperial coins, so that trade could continue.[68]

When the coins decreased in value, the risk in trading increased, resulting in higher interest rates because the risk of lending money was greater. It appears that the demand for loans (money) also decreased because interest rates were too high. Although we do not know with certainty what happened, it is reasonable to assume that trade in goods stagnated because of the high interest rates; we can also assume this happened because as mentioned we know that trade between India and the Roman Empire stagnated during this period. It was only much later, in the Byzantine period, after the establishment of the Eastern Roman Empire, that the trade resumed (again indicated by the discovery of contemporary Roman coins in India).

Reflection

The financial problems and difficulties of changing the tax system meant that the empire deliberately manipulated monetary policy. It was the emperors' financial needs which resulted in monetary units being devalued. When political and military tensions increased, the emperor had to have enough money to pay his troops. It was then natural to reduce the content of precious metal in the coins. In this way, the emperor had more money at his disposal. However, this increased supply of money resulted in higher prices, i.e. inflation. The point in this context is that there was a time-lag from the de-valuing of the coinage to when this had an impact on prices, and it was during this time-lag that those with knowledge of what was happening were able to make profits.

The link between war and inflation is well documented from the third century.[69] There was no opportunity for the empire to borrow money because it represented the "global world" at the time, and thus there was no other external entity they could borrow from. One may say that they invented another method, namely to produce more money by simply

---

[68] Rostovtzeff (1998: 472).
[69] Corbier (2005: 390).

minting more coins. When the system is large and the time-lag for information about these operations is also great, then such a procedure may be considered as a loan "from the future", because the consequences in terms of inflation come only later on.

In Gogol's novel *Dead Souls,* the protagonist, Chichikov, uses precisely this time-lag to enrich himself. Today, one may say that this time-lag is known as insider trading. However, it was probably the Romans who first discovered how to benefit from this time-lag between an action and its consequences.

The economic conditions, political chaos and military anarchy of the third century had consequences for the social conditions in the Roman Empire. We have quantitative figures to describe the social situation in the third century. We know that demand decreased, the urban population also decreased and that people moved to rural areas. We also know that the Roman Empire was devastated by civil wars during much of the third century. Much of what we know about the economic conditions is the result of studies of monetary units and taxes.

We also know something of the authors who wrote while the crisis unfolded, such as Dio Cassius. The social crisis can be inferred from his use of apocalyptic terminology about the times he wrote in. We also know something from recent archaeology.[70]

However, we know very little about the number of inhabitants of the Roman Empire in general, and especially in the third century.[71] One can, nevertheless, assume that the economic crisis, invasions, civil wars and plagues resulted in a sharp decrease in the population of the empire in the third century. Examples of the plague we know of in this context include the "Antonine" plague that ravaged Rome in AD 165–180 under the Emperor Marcus Aurelius; it is believed that the plague was brought to Rome by soldiers who had fought in Asia Minor. Another example is the "St. Cyprian Plague" which ravaged the Roman Empire between AD 250 and 270, and must also have reduced the population; we know, for example, that Emperor Claudius II Gothicus died of the plague in AD 270. However, there are no figures on how many people died in these two

[70] Corbier (2005: 395).
[71] Bagnall & Frier (1994).

plagues. However, we have figures concerning the number of deaths in Egypt, and data from Egypt may indicate something about the developments in the rest of the Roman Empire. In Egypt roughly 20 % of the population died of the "Antonine" plague. By the beginning of the third century, however, the population of Egypt had returned to its pre-plague level.[72]

We also know that around two thirds of Roman settlements in Gaul were abandoned between the second and fourth centuries. Little is known, however, about the causes of this development. There may have been several reasons: plagues, changes in production methods in agriculture, the tax burden causing farmers to abandon the land, huge debt burdens, raids by bands of robbers, invaders, etc.[73] We also know that the number of taxpayers dropped drastically between AD 178 and the beginning of the third century.[74] This may have been due to the plague, but may also have been because many tenants abandoned agriculture.[75] This may explain why Constantine the Great in a law of AD 336 forbade tenants and farmers to leave the place where they were born.[76] This law may characterise the beginning of the transition from free to bound tenant; an institution Europe struggled with in different forms and under different names until the beginning of the twentieth century. Constantine's law of AD 336 can therefore be regarded as an institutional innovation which lasted 1500 years.

It was not just the economy that stagnated in the third century. Roman literature also seems to have come to an end with Tacitus[77] and Juvenal.[78] The Roman Empire was in many respects in the third century a shadow of what it once had been. The civil wars had removed many of the empire's potential leaders. The new provinces demanded their own leaders. Many

---

[72] Rathbone (1990: 103–142); Bagnall & Frier (1994: 175–176).
[73] Hauken (1988).
[74] Bagnall & Frier (1994: 174).
[75] Bagnall & Frier (1994: 174).
[76] Corbier (2005: 400).
[77] Tacitus lived between AD 56 and 120.
[78] Juvenal lived during the end of the first century and the beginning of the second century AD.

leading families of Rome were also forced to emigrate due to the civil wars, which further emptied the city of potential leaders.[79]

Figure 2.1 shows the relationship between innovations, social mechanisms and the crisis in the third century.

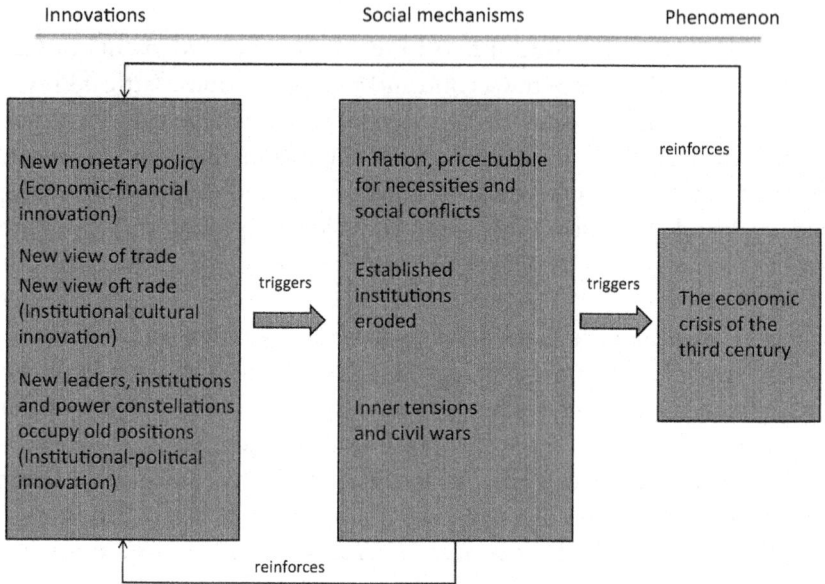

Fig. 2.1 The Long Crisis of the third century

---

[79] Frank (2005: 479).

3

The Tulip Crisis of 1637

Introduction

One February day in 1637[1], a Dutch merchant, Koestler, paid 6650 guilders for a bunch of tulip bulbs.[2] This was a huge sum of money at a time when the average family could live for a year on an income of 300 guilders.[3] How was this possible? How could a few tulip bulbs be sold for such an enormous price? In other words, the price paid by Koestler would provide approximately 20 years' income for an average Dutch family. It was not as if Koestler was a lover of flowers or intended to plant the tulip bulbs so he could enjoy the sight of the flowers when they bloomed in the following spring. No, he was a merchant who intended to make a large profit by re-selling them. However, no one had seen the

---

[1] Goldgar (2007: 1).

[2] **The tulip legend:** According to legend, the tulip originated in ancient Persia, and concerns a young couple in love. Tragedy struck when the young woman was killed by robbers. In his despair the young man rode his horse straight off a cliff and died. The blood of the young man ran into the soil, where later there grew beautiful red flowers that no one had ever seen before; these were the first tulips. The flowers have a shape resembling a turban and originate from the Persian word "turban": *toliban*.

[3] Dash (2010: xv).

© The Author(s) 2017
J.-A. Johannessen, *Innovations Lead to Economic Crises*,
DOI 10.1007/978-3-319-41793-6_3

"economic bubble" coming. In fact, few people have the ability to know when an economic bubble is developing; many bubbles burst before and after the tulip bubble.

It is only when an economic bubble bursts that it is possible to speak of an economic and social crisis. However, being able to describe *how* an economic bubble bursts does not necessarily provide insight into its causes. Detailed descriptions of the tulip bubble have been given by Goldgar[4] and Dash[5] as well as Mackay.[6] Mackay is perhaps the closest in providing an explanation of its causes; he describes the organisational and financial innovations, but without linking these to the development of the bubble.[7]

In a four-year period (1633–1637) there was a drastic rise in the price of tulip bulbs, especially between the summer of 1636 and February 1637.[8] Many people had become very rich from trading in those small tulip bulbs. Indeed, the more people who became rich, the more who were attracted into the tulip market in order to share in the wealth created.[9] What was the rationale behind the fact that so-called "reasonable people" could buy a bunch of tulip bulbs for a sum of money equal to an average family's 20-year income? Was it madness or mania; or was it an extremely skewed distribution of income; or were there other reasons that drove people to trade in tulip bulbs?

One week after Koestler had paid such a huge sum for his bunch of tulip bulbs, prices fell everywhere. Had people suddenly gained special insight into the market? Perhaps it may be presumed that Koestler had exceeded an invisible threshold, and when this threshold was breached, a so-called "dam" collapsed. In other words, confidence in the market was weakened, so that the market changed state almost from one day to the next after this invisible threshold had been exceeded.

---

[4] Goldgar (2007).

[5] Dash (2010).

[6] Mackay (1995), first published in 1841. Mackay provides an explanation of the development of the crisis, not its origins. He reasons that the development of the economic bubble was due to mass hysteria.

[7] Mackay (1995: 92–95), see especially p.93 last paragraph.

[8] Goldgar (2007: 1–2).

[9] Goldgar (2007: 194–253).

In just a few days, the price of tulip bulbs had fallen to approximately 10 % of their former value. However, even at the newly reduced prices, an average family could live for roughly two years for what a bunch of tulip bulbs cost. But by the end of 1637, the "Tulip Kings", who had been amongst the richest men in the Netherlands before the crash, at least on paper, went bankrupt and lost everything they owned.[10]

The Tulip bubble was able to expand because although investors had little of their own funds, they were able to borrow on the money market. This was also the case for Koestler: he invested 820 guilders of his own money, and borrowed a further 5830 guilders from the bank. Consequently, when prices collapsed, he was unable to pay back the money. When enough people ended up in the same financial situation it was not only confidence in the tulip market that collapsed. The banks that had lent money in the hope of making a profit also collapsed. The crisis spread, and when the tulip bubble burst many people outside the tulip market itself were left bankrupt.[11]

How could this happen? How can one explain the tulip bubble? How could the Dutch society, which had experienced tremendous success with its Dutch East India Company (VOC),[12] be tricked and duped into participating in the tulip bubble? Or is it perhaps in the very success of the Dutch East India Company where an explanation of the tulip bubble can be found?

In the Netherlands and surrounding countries there were many critics who spoke out about the extremely high prices of tulip bulbs, often in a satirical manner. However, these satirical works had little impact on the speculators who participated in the tulip bubble, and who paid no attention to warnings.[13] There have been some, albeit few, explanations of the tulip crisis. As mentioned above, one of these is Mackay,[14] who explains the crisis as a type of "herd madness", meaning that sometimes a mass of people can behave in an irrational manner. Mass psychosis may explain

---

[10] Dash (2010: xvi).

[11] Goldgar (2007: 253–305).

[12] VOC (Dutch: Vereenigde Oost-Indische Compagnie (United East India Company), i.e. the Dutch East India Company.

[13] Dash (2010: xvii).

[14] Mackay (1995).

part of the behaviour, once the bubble had been set in motion, but what explains the bubble's origins? The mass psychosis idea does little or nothing to address that problem. In other words, it is not a very satisfactory explanation that Mackay provides that the land was possessed by madness, that they were acting crazily, etc.[15]

We have little knowledge of how the tulip crisis affected the Dutch economy in this period. But the Dutch flower industry is well known today, commanding 70 % of world production and 90 % of the international trade.[16]

First, I will discuss some of the background for the tulip bubble. Second, I will discuss the development of the tulip bubble. Third, I will analyse the crisis on the basis of the selected perspective here, which is that innovations leads to economic crises.

Background

When the VOC[17] was founded, a war of independence was underway between the Dutch provinces and Spain; seven provinces joined forces in the liberation struggle, and they formed a confederation that was governed by the "States General"[18] (who are what is referred to below when state intervention is mentioned).[19]

In the case of the VOC, the state intervened for the first time in history for the benefit of shareholders.[20] If the state itself is a majority shareholder, then new issues concerning legitimacy and confidence in those running a company will also appear on the agenda.[21]

[15] Goldgar (2007: 3).

[16] Goldgar (2007: 1).

[17] The English East India Company (EIC) was established as a joint-stock association of English merchants in 1600, two years before the VOC (The Dutch East India Company). The point in this context is that a stock exchange was not established in England until several decades later (1698), although it was possible to trade in shares in the company from 1657. Like the VOC, the EIC had a monopoly on trade in the East Indies (Nordenflycht 2011: 94).

[18] Israel (2008).

[19] The Netherlands first became independent in 1648 (Jongh 2011: 63).

[20] Koppell (2011: 1–6).

[21] Koppell (2011: 11).

The Dutch West India Company was established in 1621. Although this company did not have the same success as the Dutch East India Company, it reinforced a certain new way of thinking, namely, that it was possible to invest in a portion of shares[22] rather than investing all their assets. In other words, it was easier to invest in a project than it had been before because the risk was lessened.

It was not only limited companies that were institutionalised in the Netherlands. Goldgar mentions the establishment of a chamber of assurance in 1598, a new law on trade in 1618, and the establishment of a public exchange bank, Wisselbanken, in 1609, as well as a new lending bank in 1614. These financial innovations[23] attracted trade, capital and business from all over Europe, writes Goldgar.[24]

This institutionalisation of commerce in the Netherlands meant more investments were possible with less risk. During this period the Spanish also took control of Antwerp, which may partially explain why the tulip bubble developed in Amsterdam.

Flower lovers and collectors of flowers also contributed to the increasing demand for tulips, driving up prices.[25] These two factors, however, in no way justify the extreme prices referred to above. The majority of the traders in tulip bulbs who drove up the prices were neither from the lowest or highest social strata, but from what today would be considered the middle classes. The middle classes' desire to partake in so-called upper class consumption is also likely to have been a contributing factor to the crisis.

Around 1600 tulips were well known and sought after in many parts of Europe. For instance, in France tulips were considered the first among all flowers, while in the Ottoman Empire it was considered to be God's

---

[22] Shareholders were called "participants" at the time. Co-ownership had existed in the past; however, the point of the VOC with regard to innovation was that one could freely sell its shares on a stock exchange. Thus it can be argued that it was the stock exchange that was new in 1602 and not the establishment of a limited liability company per se. But in this context it was really the relationship between the company and the stock exchange that was an innovation in 1602.

[23] Financial innovations are a subgroup of product innovations, which in turn are a subgroup of material innovations.

[24] Goldgar (2007: 9).

[25] Dash (2010: 73–122); Goldgar (2007: 62–194).

chosen flower.[26] Its popularity meant that botanists and flower lovers strived to create many different types of tulips in various colours and shades. It is estimated that by about 1600, there were approximately 100 different types of tulips; by 1630 this had increased to 1000. Long before the tulip bubble developed, tulips were being bought and sold at relatively high prices to collectors, who acquired the tulips not so much to trade with, but rather to admire the beauty of the flower's intense colour range. During the 1500s there were many tulip collectors throughout all of Europe who bought and sold tulip bulbs within a narrow circle of flower connoisseurs. When the young King Louis the 13th married, it was the height of fashion for women to adorn their clothing with cut tulips.[27]

A very special tulip bulb, Semper Augustus, was considered to be extremely beautiful. Around 1624, it was said that there existed only 12 specimens of this bulb in Amsterdam. The owner was bombarded with offers to sell the bulbs, but he refused all offers; of course, this led to new offers being made at even higher prices.[28] After being pressed to sell for a prolonged period, he was finally persuaded to sell one bulb of the Semper Augustus for 1000 guilders,[29] roughly the income of an average family for a period of three years. This may sound like a huge sum, but it must be remembered that this market was only for so-called connoisseurs of flowers. From this point on, the Semper Augustus became available to the collectors who could afford to buy it. However, this had little or nothing to do with the actual economic bubble that occurred later, because it only concerned a very small portion of a particular market and a very specific bulb. The high price of this tulip bulb lays the foundation for a greater demand for a product that was extremely inaccessible; nonetheless, the actual bubble did not take off until the market expanded beyond this connoisseurs' milieu.

Around 1630, there were tulip growers in all the villages and towns in the Netherlands. Although many grew the flower in their gardens, there

[26] Dash (2010: 73).
[27] Dash (2010: 74).
[28] Dash (2010: 94).
[29] Op. cit.

were few who cultivated them for sale. A large variety of tulip types were sold, some considered more beautiful and rare than others.[30] At the top end of the tulip market, as mentioned above, was the Semper Augustus; below this there was a hierarchy of types and prices. For instance, after Semper Augustus came a tulip named Viceroy and then the "Root en Gheel van Leyde". Below these there were countless other tulip types and prices. In other words, the tulip market at the time was not unlike other markets, where location and size were important in determining prices. Every market, even the tulip market, has a hierarchy of types and prices. The hierarchy in the tulip market was important because price increases in one category in the hierarchy could influence prices in other categories. For instance, if the price increases at the bottom of a hierarchy, then it is also likely that prices will increase further up in that hierarchy. If the market becomes opaque, traders could easily be swayed by rumours in the market and would often trade quickly to avoid ending up holding the losing cards. Timing, time lag and the degree of transparency are thus important factors in such a hierarchical market.[31]

A potential market for making large profits will of necessity attract individuals and entrepreneurs looking to make a killing. This was also the case in the tulip market at the time. The skills of the traditional, professional gardeners were important in building up the tulip market, but it grew considerably once it was exposed to the business skills of entrepreneurs. This may be considered as the "turning point" in any market, i.e. the point at which entrepreneurs enter a market area that has until then been dominated by innovators. While innovation creates disequilibrium and gaps in a market, entrepreneurs re-establish equilibrium in a market. The entrepreneurs enter the market and fill the gaps, profiting from this. This is exactly what happened in the tulip market. Around 1635, two years before the bubble burst, entrepreneurs began to make profits in the tulip market.[32] Until then the market had been limited to connoisseurs and professional "flower lovers". Now the market was taken over by

---

[30] Dash (2010: 96).

[31] For those who do not immediately see that complexity and time lag are social mechanisms in such a market, Gogol's *Dead Souls* is recommended; he has thoroughly understood complexity and time lag in all markets.

[32] Dash (2010: 91–109).

entrepreneurs or "profit lovers". It is at this point that the bubble takes flight; it doesn't burst, it just expands. And it is from this point the words "hysteria", "mania", "irrationality", "madness", "greed" and "tulip-fools" are used. The truth is that it was the "profit lovers" who took over the market from the "flower lovers".

The Development of the Bubble

I first describe how the tulip bubble developed; then I examine how it burst.

The Bubble Develops

The Amsterdam stock exchange was established in 1602 as a means of paving the way for the expansion of the Dutch East India Company (VOC).[33] This was an important social mechanism that enabled the bubble to take off in 1636–1637; it was introduced as an institutional innovation in Amsterdam and other Dutch cities; and was an innovation that was to have enormous consequences not only for the Dutch economy, but for the entire world. The advent of stock exchanges made it possible for anyone to invest in a limited liability company[34]; investment risk was lessened because investors only risked their initial investment. Before the advent of this innovation, investors could risk losing their entire fortune, if things went wrong.

The stock exchanges in Haarlem, Leyden, Alkmar, Hoorn and other towns in the Netherlands[35] became venues for financial speculation.

---

[33] The first English joint-stock company, the Virginia Company of London (VCL), was established in 1606 (Hall 2011: 123). The reasons this innovation did not lead to a "tulip bubble" in England are following. First, the company was not a success for shareholders and it closed in 1624. Second, a stock exchange was not established in England until 1698, when the London Stock Exchange was established. Similarly, a "tulip bubble" did not occur in France, because the first limited liability company was not established until roughly 1664, and there was no stock exchange in France during this period; however, the facts are unclear here because the bulk of the first French limited liability company's documents have been lost (Dibadj 2011: 169).

[34] In England a stock exchange was established almost one hundred years later in 1698.

[35] Mackay (1995: 93).

These exchanges acted as a driving force in the development of the tulip bubble. When banks also saw a profit opportunity in lending money to investors on the stock exchange, a financial opportunity was coupled with an institutional innovation.

In addition to the two institutional innovations—the stock exchange and the limited liability company—a new financial product was also introduced in the loan market, called "Windhandel" ("Wind Trade"). Wind Trade may best be described as being similar to today's "futures". This new financial product, which was a financial innovation, reinforced the effect of the two institutional innovations mentioned above.

The Tulip Bubble may also in some sense be considered as a type of gambling craze,[36] where many people saw the opportunity to make big money fast. The result of such a collective strategy is a huge price increase for the good in demand. There was rampant speculation on the stock exchanges in the various Dutch towns as the stock prices of tulip bulbs rose and fell in price (via Wind Trade). Large profits were made when the stock prices fell for tulip bulbs, and similarly when the stock prices rose.[37] Many people became unimaginably rich overnight, as if they had discovered their own personal gold mine—which they had, in a figurative sense. An assumption that Mackay makes, and which seems to be correct, is that those who acted in the tulip market were under the delusion that it would last forever. Mackay further writes that it was imagined that poverty would disappear from the Netherlands, and that wealth would spread to all the social strata of the population. When such thinking prevails, why would anyone want to wear themselves out in ordinary jobs producing tangible goods and services? The nobility, city dwellers, craftsmen and tradesmen, sailors, servants and even chimney sweeps, yes, all kinds of people, seized the opportunity to partake in this newfound wealth. Anyone with any kind of assets, such as a house, land or a boat, could convert these through the new credit instruments of the banks into money, which could then be invested on the stock exchanges. Prices rose, time passed, and everyone earned good money for a period of time. Of course, the thinking goes, once you have made a bit of money, why not try

---

[36] Mackay (1995: 93).
[37] Mackay (1995: 94).

and make a little more? People elsewhere in Europe saw that people were accumulating wealth in this manner in the Netherlands; consequently, foreign capital flowed into the country to join in this dance around the golden calf. An interesting side note is that when the price of a luxury good, in this case tulip bulbs, rises, then other luxury goods, such as riding horses and fine carriages, also rise in price.[38] Although there were no stock exchanges in the smaller towns, there were markets where tulip bulbs and money changed hands directly.

When something is too good to be true, then it probably isn't true, as the saying goes. Under such conditions it is usually wise to re-assess the situation in hand. However, in the case of the tulipmania simple common sense seems to have been completely ignored. It was as if there was a kind of collective blindness: people wanted to be where money was being earned. When it was rumoured that it was possible to make money, big money, buying and selling tulip bulbs, then traders flocked to Amsterdam from towns throughout the Netherlands, as well as from other places in Europe. Between 1635 and February 1637, prices increased dramatically, making some people very rich. Some people managed to get out of the market before the bubble burst, while others, both the newly rich and established wealthy families, went bankrupt.

The structure of any bubble is initially held together partly by the trust placed in "people of honour".[39] This is because the vast majority of those who invested in the tulip bubble—or other bubbles—did not only use their own funds. They invested their own capital, but this may have represented only, say, 10 % of the total amount invested; the remaining 90 % would have been borrowed from banks or moneylenders. As long as everyone is raking in money at a canter, and there is confidence in a market, then more people will enter the market. When more people enter the market, then those involved can make more money, both the buyers and sellers of goods—in this case tulip bulbs—as well as those lending money to investors. As long as prices rise, then the money will continue to flow. In such a zeitgeist, the feeling is that you have to invest to make a profit. The point in this context is that trust and confidence are usually

---

[38] Mackay (1995: 94).
[39] Goldgar (2007: 196).

fragile—in this case, it was based on the idea that the price of tulip bulbs would keep on rising. When the turnaround comes, confidence evaporates and the so-called "people of honour" are often concerned more with their own welfare than with the solvency of the banks and lending institutions. After the bubble bursts, the lesson is learnt the hard way in the form of losses, bankruptcy and personal disasters.

In 1612, the price of tulip bulbs varied between 10 and 25 guilders[40]; before the bubble burst some 25 years later, the price was roughly 6650 guilders! There is no general overview of the price development of tulips between 1620 and 1635, other than the indication we have of prices in 1612. However, we know that a collector in 1625 was offered 2000–3000 guilders for some Semper Augustus tulip bulbs. In 1635, there are some records of purchases and sales, but they are nowhere near the price the Semper Augustus bulbs achieved. "Saeyblom van Coningh" and another type of tulip bulb, "Latour", were sold respectively for 30 guilders and 27 guilders.[41] This gives us an idea of the extremely high prices offered when we know that an average Dutch family could live on an annual income of 300 guilders!

In 1636, tulip bulbs were a hot topic on the Dutch market. A sense of collective optimism was reported from several places in the market in the Netherlands.[42] Optimism and excitement about this new product spread to more and more areas. Consequently, more people entered the market in order to make money. Around 1636, it was not only the Semper Augustus bulb that rose in price, but all kinds of other tulip bulbs too. In late 1636, the more luxurious tulip bulbs, such as "Viceroy", "Admiral van Enkhuizen", "Switser" and "Admiral Lieffkens", also began to command very high prices. These now took their places in the top of the tulip hierarchy just below the "Semper Augustus". "Switser", for instance, rose from a price of 125 guilders per pound on 31 December 1636 to a price of 1500 guilders per pound on 3 February 1637.[43] It seems at this point in time that there was a relationship between collective optimism and the

---

[40] Goldgar (2007: 197).
[41] Goldgar (2007: 201).
[42] Goldgar (2007: 202).
[43] Goldgar (2007: 202).

development of collective blindness. Before the bubble burst, there were stories such as that from 1633, when a handful of tulip bulbs were used as payment for a house and a piece of agricultural land in Friesland.[44] Such transactions show that the tulip bulb had a particularly high value at least four years before the crisis. In hindsight, this transaction is a sign that a bubble was developing, although no one could see it when it actually happened. Dash writes that a house with farmland in Friesland would have been sold for not less than 500 guilders, which gives us an idea of the price of tulip bulbs at that time.[45] It could not have been the "Semper Augustus" that was sold on that occasion, because they were not for sale then; based on the prices of houses and farmland, it was probably tulip bulbs of medium value.

It may be said that the turnaround came after the flower season in 1635, in the autumn, when a trade innovation was introduced, writes Dash[46]; from this point on, other players besides the professional tulip growers enter the market, namely the entrepreneurs who saw opportunities for making profits. In the Netherlands, this change coincides with emergence of the Wind Trade mentioned above; this expression has a figurative meaning that refers to the strong winds on the coast of the Netherlands that send trade in the direction it blows. The term symbolises the collective mania that took hold of the tulip market, like a ship sailing where the wind blows.

Towards the end of 1634, the prices of tulip bulbs increased. But now it was no longer only the most valuable tulips that rose in price; all types of tulip bulbs began to achieve higher market values. Between December 1636 and February 1637, certain types of tulip bulbs doubled in value in just one week.[47] In retrospect, of course, it is possible to say that people should have been able to see that the bubble was about to burst. However, at the time people were not able to "see" this. The prices kept increasing in value until February 1637. In December 1636 and January 1637 the bubble expanded, but it did not burst. On the con-

---

[44] Friesland is a province in the north and west of the Netherlands and includes an archipelago.
[45] Dash (2010: 123).
[46] Dash (2010: 132).
[47] Dash (2010: 124).

trary, merchants from all over the Netherlands flocked to take part in this adventure. For two months everyone earned big money. Increased demand led to higher prices, which rose for all kinds of tulips. However, as mentioned above, the money that flowed to the stock exchanges was largely borrowed money. If one managed to sell, one could make large profits. People borrowed more to make more. The carousel continued to spin around and around. This went very well for two months, then the bubble burst one day in February 1637. Everyone now involved in the trade had the major part of their investments outstanding in loans, while the banks had outstanding claims for unfathomable amounts. The whole market collapsed, and confidence disappeared, while the banks tried to claw their money back. But as we know, nothing can be gained when there is nothing to be had. Thus, it was not only those who had speculated on the prices of tulip bulbs who went bankrupt: trading companies and banks also collapsed.

When prices stabilise for a period before they start going down, this indicates that some investors have realised "that the emperor has no clothes", and they try to get out safely before the bubble bursts. But confidence is destroyed, and panic begins. These are clear signs that the bubble is going to burst. The first thing that happened when confidence collapsed in the Netherlands was that the various representatives of the many towns gathered and went to the central government. There, they proposed that the government do something to re-establish confidence in the tulip market.[48]

Analysis

Six innovations are discussed in the following, which are related to what subsequently occurred, i.e. the growth of the tulip bubble and its eventual bursting (1635–1637). These six are the following: The first is the establishment of limited liability companies. The second is the creation of the first stock exchange, where securities, rather than actual goods of real value, could be freely traded. The third is the assumption that political

---

[48] Mackay (1995: 95).

innovations created expectations and attitudes in the population, which may partly explain the tulipmania. The fourth is the flower itself, i.e. the tulip, which was a product innovation in the Dutch market. The fifth is the "Windhandel" (Wind Trade), which was similar to today's "futures". The sixth innovation is the adoption and dominance of the mercantilist doctrine and policies in Europe.

The World's First Joint Stock Company is Established in 1602: An Institutional Innovation

Today, we often read and hear about leaders who are paid disproportionately high salaries, of dividends that are not paid or are small, and about inside trading, etc. These phenomena are by no means new, but those that have followed companies since day one of their first appearance, which was in 1602. As early as 1609, no shareholders had received dividends from the VOC. After a shareholder, Isaac Le Maire, wrote a letter of protest on the 24th January 1609 to the Netherlands' most influential politician at the time, Johan van Oldenbarnvelt, the government intervened. After this political intervention in the private company, the VOC paid 18–20 % dividend on stock capital from 1610 up until when the company went bankrupt in 1800.[49] The protest explained that the lack of dividend payments was due to the fact that the Board paid large salaries to management. This protest from one single shareholder may be viewed as the world's first shareholder revolt against a company. From another perspective, the episode may also be viewed as the first government intervention in what may be termed "corporate governance".[50] It may also be understood as an important origin of what is known as "principal-agent" problems.[51]

The VOC was formed by wealthy merchants who had traded in the East Indies between 1594 and 1602. Voyages to the East Indies during this period were high risk ventures; the owners, who could be part-

---

[49] Koppell (2011: 1–6).

[50] "Corporate governance" may be described as "the system by which companies are directed and controlled" (Aglietta, M. & A. Rebérioux 2005: 77).

[51] Fama (1980: 288); Jensen & Meckling (1976).

owners of a ship, risked losing the whole cargo and thus everything they had invested in a trading voyage. The new feature of the VOC, as an institutional innovation, was that in principle, the so-called maid, the farmer and public employee, could also be part-owners in the same way, though not to the same extent, as the rich merchant who had earlier carried out trade in the East Indies. Previously, it was the skipper and owner and a few merchants who had joined together to invest and organise single trading voyages. If anything went wrong on these voyages, they risked bankruptcy and social disaster. With the VOC's many ships, the possibility of a total loss was less likely, and the voyages were less hazardous, amongst other things, because the VOC could use military support; this was a political innovation, where the government had intervened through the "States General" [52] and granted the VOC with the authority to use armed force when defending itself.

The World's First Stock Exchange: An Institutional, Political Innovation

After the establishment of the Dutch stock exchange, the VOC's stocks could be freely traded.[53] This innovation made it possible to separate ownership from management. Before the advent of limited companies, ownership and management had largely been a single unit. Now this unit could be divided into what is known today as "principal" and "agent". Gelderblom et al. argue that stocks in companies also existed before 1602; these were in reality not so much stocks, but rather part shares of say a ship, company or trading activity.[54] One may consider these part shares in a trading activity or ship as stocks before 1602, but nevertheless, they could not be freely traded. It is the link between stocks and a stock exchange that is new and innovative in 1602, and it is this institutional innovation which affected the economy, in this case the tulip bubble in the Netherlands.

---

[52] Jongh (2011: 82–83), note 5.
[53] Gelderblom et al. (2011: 30).
[54] Gelderblom et al. (2011: 36–37).

The institutions that were built up to develop trade were, according to North, the foundation of the modern Western economy.[55] The stock exchange (est. 1602) was such an institutional innovation. An important point in this connection is that people had a belief in state intervention in relation to this innovation, because the Dutch "States General" had granted the VOC monopoly trading rights and the right to use military force. This may have led to the idea that people believed that if something went wrong, then the state would step in and take control. This may also provide one of the explanations why the tulip bubble grew. People had confidence that the state would be the guarantor of success.

Another financial innovation was the creation of the Amsterdam Bank in 1609,[56] which made trade easier and the trading of shares more efficient. The bank could also function as an intermediate trader and provide loans to those who bought shares in what a little later was termed "Windhandel" (Wind Trade). Between 1609 and 1621 large sums were accumulated in the Amsterdam Bank. The whole of the Dutch capital market exploded and capital accumulated.[57] The capital sought profit opportunities when trading activities grew around 1625. The fuel for the bubble can then be thought to have come from the accumulated capital seeking profit opportunities. The success of the Amsterdam Bank led to the establishment of several other banks in the Netherlands and Germany.[58]

In addition to the Amsterdam Bank, a number of financial techniques also arrived in Amsterdam and the Netherlands.[59] One of these techniques, which may at first glance seem like a curiosity, may possibly explain something of the tulip bubble's development. Schama[60] writes that one of the techniques that you learned in Amsterdam, which had come from Antwerp, was gambling. The love of gambling[61] was one of

[55] North (1990).
[56] Israel (1991)
[57] Lambert (1971: 186).
[58] Kindleberger (1996: 97).
[59] Kindleberger (1996: 96).
[60] Schama (1988: 347–350).
[61] Schama (1988: 503–505).

the traits Schama found when looking at the Dutch during the period in question. This may also partly explain the tulip bubble's development.

The VOC was Granted the Right to Use Military Power: An Institutional, Political Innovation

The VOC was allowed to maintain military units. The company also had a monopoly on the trade in spices, especially pepper. The company was also granted the right to administer colonies and mint coins.

Although the VOC was the first private joint stock company in the world, there is much to suggest that the structure was more of a private—public partnership.[62] This makes the VOC just as much a political innovation as an organisational innovation. With the state as a partner, the VOC could deal with challenges in the East Indies in completely different ways than a purely private company was able to do. This political innovation allowed the VOC to erect strong military forts along the whole of the trade route in the East Indies. The success of the company may also be understood from the perspective of being a political innovation, where a private—public structure produced revenue for both the shareholders (after 1610) and the Dutch government.[63] The VOC was a private corporation, which also performed public tasks, military and judicial activities in the areas the company operated in. Specifically, the company fought against the Portuguese and Spanish in the colonies that the company had established in the East Indies.[64] "Bleeding the Spanish resources"[65] was an aim in this context. A political innovation of this kind was something that was quite exceptional at the time.

However, the VOC was by no means the first company that traded and sailed ships to the East Indies. From 1595 to 1601, 66 ships sailed from Amsterdam, Middelburg and Rotterdam to the East Indies to trade.[66] What is relevant here though is that these companies were not limited

---

[62] Gelderblom et al. (2011: 30).
[63] Op. cit.
[64] Israel (1991: 70–72).
[65] Gelderblom et al. (2011: 47).
[66] Gelderblom et al. (2011: 36).

companies, nor had they been granted military powers by the government, other than the right to protect themselves against thieves and pirates.

A separate public ministry could have been established in the Netherlands to take care of the East Indies trade; such a ministry existed, for instance, in Spain, so it would not have been controversial. However, the Dutch authorities through the "States General" chose to do things differently: public control was established in the foundation meeting and laid down in the VOC's charter".[67] Out of the 46 articles of the charter, 29 were concerned with the relationship between state governance and shareholders' rights.[68] Some of these articles included the rights to establish colonial agreements, declare war and mint money. On the basis of the charter, it is reasonable to call the VOC a "semi-public enterprise".[69] Compared with the public interest and the interests of the company's leadership, the investors' interests, i.e. the shareholders, was relatively small. In our context, however, this led to a greater confidence that the government would intervene if something happened to the detriment of the shareholders' interests. This was also the case in 1609 as mentioned above when a shareholder asked the authorities to intervene concerning the non-payment of dividends. It may be imagined that this reliance on governmental intervention also spilled over into the stock exchange, which was another innovation at the time. If this assumption is correct, then it partly explains why the tulip bubble could develop as it did.

The War of Independence against Spain also meant that the seven Dutch provinces had an interest in merging the Dutch merchants into a unified East Indies trading company, so they would be able to stand stronger against the Spaniards, who also traded in the East Indies. The "States General", i.e. the public authority that governed the seven provinces that fought against Spain, gave the VOC monopoly of trade in the East Indies.[70]

In plain language, this political innovation followed the tenets of mercantilist doctrine. Monopolies and privileges were granted to the VOC, and the company was granted the right by the state to carry out mili-

---

[67] Israel (2008).
[68] Gelderblom et al. (2011: 40).
[69] Gelderblom, et al. (2011: 44).
[70] Jongh (2011: 63.

tary actions if necessary. The purpose was to promote a trade surplus, because mercantilism espouses that the nations that export more than they import are winners in economic terms.[71]

The Tulip: An Economic, Product Innovation

The tulip is originally a flower from Central Asia, possibly Persia, according to myth. It is also possible that it originates from areas north of the Himalayas, in the Tien Shan Mountains along China's western border. The original flower was smaller than the one we know today, because it had adapted to the cold conditions in the mountains. The original colour was red. The flower wandered westward with traders and warriors. The first time we hear about it in the West is from Persian myths around 1050. Then we hear of tulips in the Ottoman Empire, and in relation to the Ottoman conquest of the Balkans from 1345. It was especially after the Ottomans defeated the Serbs on the Kosovo Plains in 1389 that the tulip could be found in the gardens in the Balkan Peninsula.[72] The reason the Ottomans spread the tulip in their campaigns is that gardens were very important to them, and the tulip was considered a sacred flower, writes Dash.[73]

The tulip bulbs first came to the Netherlands around 1593[74] with a traveller, Jan Somer, who brought them from Constantinople and Italy.[75] Not unsurprisingly, the tulip bulbs were first transported to the Netherlands via Antwerp, one of the most important trading cities in Europe at the time. Jan Somer had a small garden outside Antwerp, on the coast of Zeeland; it was there that the first tulips bloomed in the Netherlands.[76] We also know that the bulbs came to northern Italy sometime between

---

[71] Magnusson (1994).

[72] Dash (2010: 14).

[73] Dash (2010: 12).

[74] There are also accounts described in Goldgar (2007: 32–34), which claim that the tulip came to the Netherlands in 1550–1583. Dash also provides an account in which he describes the tulip blooming for the first time in 1559 (Dash 2010: 36). However, the point in this context is not the exact date of the arrival of the tulip bulb and their flowering in the Netherlands, but the fact that the tulip bubble did not burst until several decades later.

[75] Goldgar (2007: 22)

[76] Goldgar (2007: 23).

1549 and 1551, to Switzerland in 1559, Austria in 1572, Frankfurt in 1593, France in 1598 and to England around 1582.[77] The point of specifying the tulip's journey through Europe is to ask the question: Why did the tulip bubble occur in the Netherlands and not in any of the other countries where the flower was also grown?

In 1630, the tulips were new to the Dutch, and they were also rare. Novelty and rarity and the fact that several people saw great potential in the product, the expectations of a Golden Age, seem to be the characteristic of the tulip bubble's origin. If we understand innovation as "any idea, practice, or material artefact perceived to be new by the relevant unit of adoption",[78] which is a widely used definition of innovation,[79] then the tulip was an innovation in the Netherlands in 1593. However, it took around 30 years before this innovation led to an economic and social crisis for many families in the Netherlands.

Over a period of time, trade changed in focus from fish, grain and timber etc. to tulip bulbs. Traditional production and trade were completely ignored while the tulip bubble developed.[80] The explanation is of course that most traders were able to share in the huge profits that these bulbs could yield.

Tulips were sold in both London and Paris for very high prices in the market.[81] Important in this context is that the tulip bubble did not develop in England or France, as it did in the Netherlands.

"Windhandel"[82] (Wind Trade): An Economic, Financial Innovation

"Windhandel" (Wind Trade) is a term the Dutch used when referring to a particular era in the tulip bubble's development.[83] As mentioned above,

---

[77] Dash (2010: 38–39).
[78] Zaltman et al. (1973).
[79] Johannessen et al. (2001: 20–31).
[80] Mackay (1995: 90).
[81] Mackay (1995: 96).
[82] Today, "Windhandel" (Wind Trade) may be compared to "futures".
[83] Dash (2010: 132).

"Wind trade" means "trading in the wind", or figuratively, putting your finger in the air to see which way the wind is blowing, and then making a decision based on what the wind tells you. This concept became a reality because you could trade on the stock exchange in the late autumn, winter and early spring, although the tulips did not bloom until after trading on the exchange was over. This can be understood as a financial innovation, where you could trade in a market, even if the goods in question did not actually exist; their value would only be realised at a later date. In other words, one traded in a future market, hence the current name of "futures". This innovation was introduced into the stock exchange in autumn 1635. We must be aware of the fact that it was precisely from 1635 onwards that the tulip bubble is thought to have developed, only to burst two years later. From autumn 1635 it was possible to buy and sell shares in a future product that was literally still "in the earth" without the knowledge of what it was going to look like the day it blossomed, i.e. the tulips. From now on it was no longer the tulip bulbs that changed hands, but the contracts concerning "future tulips". Both assumptions about the future product and expectations about the future market were now brought in as two crucial elements of the tulip market in the Netherlands.

The advantage of such a system was that the trade could take place even if the goods did not yet exist. The disadvantages or dangers were of course that the goods would not be realised, or that the market had changed totally in character by the time the tulip bulbs and money were to change hands. The duty of disclosure did not exist either, so the buyer could not know whether the bulbs belonged to the seller or if the bulbs even existed. This of course opened the market for criminal minds, who also entered the market at this time. Dash writes about this innovation as follows: "It was this innovation that made the greatest excess of the mania possible."[84] Dash then relates innovation to future financial crises, without reflecting on this claim; he does not go back into the past to examine the institutional innovations that were created around the VOC, and how these may have affected the tulip bubble's development.

It is reasonable to believe that confidence in limited companies and the "Wind Trade" can be traced to government intervention in the

---

[84] Dash (2010: 132).

VOC as early as in 1609, where the state through the "States General" secured shareholders' dividends with approximately 20 % from 1610 and throughout its history. It is also reasonable to assume that this confidence in state intervention may have reinforced the "Wind Trade" market.

Mercantilism's Breakthrough: Institutional Innovation

The mercantilist doctrine, which was a political-economic way of thinking in the 1500s–1700s, had the following characteristics: The state promoted monopolies, where they had ownership or significant influence, as was the case with the VOC. Private companies were granted government privileges. One example was the right to use military power, colonise territories and mint money—all privileges which the Dutch government had granted the VOC.

An important tenet of the mercantile doctrine was to promote trade and increase exports and reduce imports. The mercantile mindset may have led to the attitudes that led investors to rely on the state to intervene and manage development, as it had done with the VOC.

Mercantilist doctrine refers to both economic thinking and trade-related policies, which promoted the intervention of government authorities. Some of the most basic ideas in the mercantilist doctrine, although it cannot be regarded as a monolithic system of thought, are the following[85]:

1. Trade and technology are critical elements of a nation's economic prosperity.
2. Industrial production and trade are more important than agricultural production for a nation's prosperity.
3. Power and intervention are important in order to take control of trade.
4. Colonisation is important for power and trade.

Export is the main element of a nation's wealth in mercantile thinking. It follows that the revenue from this trade, i.e. gold and silver, is the main evidence of a country's prosperity. To achieve this, exports are promoted, and imports restricted.

---

[85] Brezis (2003: 483).

Mercantilist doctrine promoted a strong state, which led to the idea that the state could intervene, if something went wrong. When the tulip crisis developed, this thinking was part of the economic reality in the Netherlands. One can assume that speculators thought the government would intervene and manage the development. This is what they did, at least in the case when they supported shareholders' concerning payment of dividends by the VOC. This may have been one of the reasons why the tulip bubble did not correct itself, but only grew and then burst.

Reflection

It is the combination of economic and institutional innovations that led to the tulip bubble's development. It is not probable that a product innovation in itself could lead to an economic bubble. It appears that institutional innovations coupled in time with an economic innovation, in this case a product innovation, the tulip, resulted in the tulip bubble, as is illustrated in Fig. 3.1.

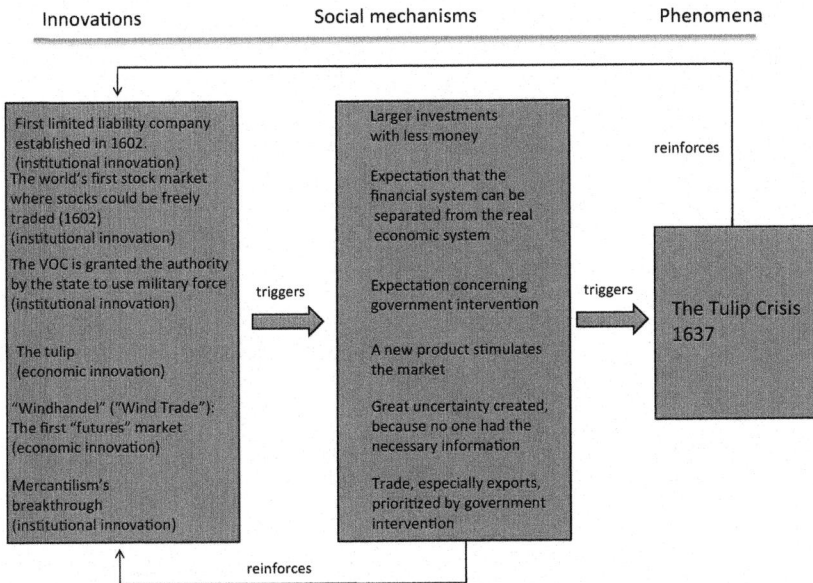

Fig. 3.1 The Tulip Crisis in 1637

The period between 1590 and 1620 in Dutch economic history is considered to be an economic miracle,[86] which can be explained in many ways. One of the explanations is the institutional and economic innovations described in this case. The same innovations that promote an economic miracle paradoxically also carry within them the seeds of an economic crisis. This may be understood as innovation's Janus face. On the one hand, Fortuna smiles, while on the other, Nemesis is ready with a crisis. This is where the Norwegian philosopher Zappfe's aphorism applies: "It's what you're good at that becomes your downfall". Zappfe's paradox appears to be a partial explanation of the relationship between innovations and economic crises.

On a theoretical level, it is possible to say that when an unknown threshold value is surpassed, this causes the market to suddenly give feedback that the upper limit has been reached. The confidence in the market then suddenly collapses. A self-reinforcing trend sets in and pushes the market towards equilibrium at a lower level. Innovation brings disequilibrium to any market. Exceeding a threshold value causes a crisis of confidence. The market explodes through self-reinforcing feedback loops. Corrections set in, and the price of the goods in question, in this case tulips, is reduced to a new equilibrium level.

---

[86] Slicher van Bath (1982: 23).

4

The South Sea and Mississippi Bubbles of 1720

Introduction

The South Sea Bubble is said to be one of the greatest scandals in financial history.[1] It has become a metaphor for deceitfulness, illusion and trickery in the financial world.[2] It is often explained from the perspective that it typifies the spirit of the times, which was characterised, amongst other things, by speculation and gambling.[3] Behavioural theory applied to financial activities[4] explains an economic bubble from a rational perspective, saying many may act irrationally, but there will be those who don't.[5] The four "classic" books on the subject of the South Sea Bubble explain the economic bubble in terms of irrational mania[6]; they view the trading activities of the South Sea Company as being insignificant. Paul disagrees with them, saying that the slave trade brought revenues to the

---

[1] Paul (2011: 1).

[2] Mackay adeptly relates bubbles to mania, irrational behaviour, illusion and trickery (Mackay 1995).

[3] Dale (2004).

[4] "Behavioural finance" uses psychological models to explain financial behaviour (Paul 2011: 5).

[5] Rational bubbles have been thoroughly explained by Tirole (1982, 1985); Garber (2000).

[6] Scott (1912); Dickson (1967); Mackay (1995); Carswell (1993).

© The Author(s) 2017
J.-A. Johannessen, *Innovations Lead to Economic Crises*,
DOI 10.1007/978-3-319-41793-6_4

company, and that these were substantial and may be an important clue as to why people bought shares in the South Sea Company. Paul's findings are important because they suggest that investors bought shares on the basis of rational expectations of increasing their income based on the company's revenues from the slave trade.

One reason why the "mania" explanation has had such an impact in all the theoretical writings about economic bubbles—including the case of the South Sea Bubble—may be that neoclassical economic theory is unable to explain the development of an economic bubble. However, it is only when the bubble is viewed "in the rear-view mirror" that people are able to argue that it was an expression of irrational mania,[7] even though the reality may well be the opposite.[8] The development of the economic bubble was rational, as Paul shows in her use of cliometric[9] data. Carlos and Neal, Temin and Voth, and Shea[10] have also demonstrated using other cliometric data that the bubble's development can be justified rationally. Although not everyone may have acted rationally, many did. Most writers today, however, claim that it was an irrational behaviour and a form of gambling mania that led to the bubble's growth. It may also be the case that the "irrational behaviour" explanation has "face value", because it is easy to "sell" to the reader.

I am not trying to claim here that innovation can explain everything in the development of an economic bubble, but rather that it can be an aspect of the explanation concerning the development of an economic crisis, including both economic bubbles and other types of crises.[11]

---

[7] The classical works concerning explanations of effective markets are, amongst others, Fama (1970, 1991). The classical works in the field of economics which argue that people can act rashly and thereby create a bubble include, amongst others, De Bondt & Thaler (1993).

[8] Neoclassical economics emphasizes the idea that markets strive for equilibrium, where supply and demand are balanced through a "correct" price. My point in this context is that an innovation will always bring a market out of equilibrium, and introduce an "innovation price". The market may strive towards equilibrium after an innovation has disrupted this equilibrium by means of entrepreneurs who fill the gap in the market which innovations have created. However, the more innovations that are introduced into the market, the more gaps that will appear in the market, bringing it out of balance. It is the rational actions that people—entrepreneurs—undertake in order to act in relation to an innovation that bring the market into equilibrium again.

[9] Cliometric research has been called the new economic history (Neal 1990).

[10] Carlos & Neal (2006); Temin & Voth (2004); Shea (2007a, b).

[11] This assumption is supported in part by Neal (1990). In Paul's book she analyses the South Sea Bubble, and touches on the importance of innovation for the development of bubbles: "...These difficulties are part of the problems of financial innovation and development." (Paul 2011: 101).

In 1720, the stock exchanges in London, Paris and Amsterdam collapsed; and those in Hamburg and Lisbon also suffered partial collapses.[12] In other words, about 90 years after the Tulip Bubble, the same thing happened again: an economic bubble developed and bursts. The Tulip, Mississippi and South Sea Bubbles all had one important pre-condition that enabled their emergence: the existence of stock exchanges, where a share could be issued by one party to another, and could also be freely sold to a third party.[13]

When the share price in the South Sea Company increased from £100 to £1000 in 1720, and dropped to £150 in September of that year, it goes without saying that those who sold out before the price fell made a great deal of money (or, in the case of the state, were able to manage the national debt).

The price of shares in the South Sea Company is also interesting in light of what we know about the average income of a family in England at this time: a lower middle class family had an income of between £15 and £50 per year.[14] When the share price was at its highest in 1720 (at £1000), such families would have been able to live for 22–66 years for the price of just one share (indicating, amongst other things, the scale of social inequality that existed in England at the time).

France and Britain both wished to rid themselves of their huge national debts, which they had accumulated due to the wars of the 1600s.[15] The South Sea Company in London undertook to convert their shares to public assets, so that deficits in the public finances would be brought under control.[16] This can be termed as a private–public financial innovation, because the government was able to cover its deficits, while a private company was able to perform its activities. The first stock exchange in

---

There are of course innovations other than the financial ones that influence the growth of an economic bubble, including amongst others, institutional innovations (Johannessen, 2014, forthcoming).

[12] Goldgar (2007: 305), Balen (2003: 1–12).

[13] Paul (2011: 44).

[14] Dale (2004: 6).

[15] Dickson (1967). War and revolutions characterise the age. The English Revolution of 1688 resulted in, amongst other things, an institutional innovation in England. The Peace of Utrecht was signed in 1713; this put an end to several European wars, amongst them the War of the Spanish Succession, which also had consequences for several European countries.

[16] Goldgar (2007: 305).

England was established in London in 1698[17]; along with the new financial loan schemes this led to increased financial speculation.

Investors from, for instance, the Netherlands travelled to London to take part in this new profit opportunity.[18] The Dutch invested in both the Paris stock exchange, in what was later called the Mississippi Bubble, and the London Stock Exchange, what later became known as the South Sea Bubble.[19] The Dutch initiated many new businesses based on the same financial loan innovations on the Amsterdam stock exchange, involving companies such as those trading in clothing, sugar and tobacco.[20] The South Sea Company also invested in the slave traffic between Africa and the new continent, America.[21]

In 1720 all these investments resulted in what Neal calls the first financial crisis,[22] which threatened both governments and the management of several large companies.

Two new innovations, the London Stock Exchange and the private–public lending instrument, made it possible for investors to be anywhere at almost any time when making investments. It obviously cannot be compared with the rapidity of today's information and communication technology, but at the time horse transport enabled a reasonably efficient means of communication for investors. The new financial instruments meant more people could invest less of their own funds, even as the sum of investments increased; the risk of losing everything one owned was reduced, but of course investors could lose the actual money they had invested.

If it is the case that it is irrational to invest in shares where the difference between the share value and the underlying value is too large, then obviously all economic bubbles are an expression of irrational behaviour.

---

[17] The London Stock Exchange was not officially opened until 1801. However, dealings of a stock exchange like nature were carried on beginning in 1698 in "Exchange Alley" and in the so-called coffee houses. In reality, shares were traded in a way similar to a regular stock exchange.

[18] Carswell (1993).

[19] Scott (1912), Vol. 3.

[20] Goldgar (2007: 306).

[21] Paul (2011: 54).

[22] Neal (1990).

This approach is adopted by Dale[23]; it is perhaps understandable that he takes this perspective, as he is a Professor of Banking, and rational investments represent a bank's legitimacy and viability. Nevertheless, there are quite a few banks throughout history that have collapsed because they have behaved "irrationally". The question in this context is not whether investments where there is a too large difference in the P/E[24] ratio are irrational, but why individuals and systems invest at all when the differences in the P/E ratio are so large?

There are many different explanations of the South Sea Bubble: everything from collective mania[25] to gambling addiction.[26] For instance, during this period it was even possible to gamble by taking out life insurance on another person,[27] which became a game where other people's lives were "at stake" (and this type of insurance was made illegal in 1774).

It may be said that the main "ingredient" in the South Sea Bubble was the government's need to reduce the national debt, and the various measures it introduced to achieve this end. Instead of levying heavy taxes, the government planned to reduce the national debt through the publicly controlled South Sea Company[28]: the company was granted a monopoly to trade with South America,[29] and private investors believed great profits could be made and so invested large sums of money. The government planned to sell its shares if the share prices rose, thus reducing the cost of the national debt.

However, the South Sea Company was not the only company that was established as a limited liability company in the early 1700s. After the London Stock Exchange came into operation, there were several companies that contributed to pushing up stock prices with promises of wealth and huge profits. The South Sea Company was partially taken over by the state and continued its management of the national debt until 1850.

---

[23] Ibid.

[24] P/E stands for the ratio of price to earnings, i.e., the share price or market value in relation to a company's income as represented through its net income.

[25] Mackay (1995).

[26] Clark (1999: 49–50).

[27] Dale (2004: 4), note 6 page 6.

[28] Sperling (1962: 1–14).

[29] Paul (2011: 54).

Other economic bubbles existed more or less simultaneously with the South Sea Bubble. For instance, the Mississippi Bubble[30] (1720) was created by the Mississippi Company in France; the company attracted investors with promises of huge profits in the French colonies in North America. The Bengal Bubble (1769) was driven by the rising shares of the British East India Company; the shares peaked when rebellion broke out in India, and then the bubble burst.

Professional stock traders ran their business mainly from one particular street in London called "Exchange Alley". Here they worked from coffee houses, received information through the rumour mill and from the London newspapers; around 1700, London had a population of roughly half a million inhabitants. Information travelled quickly between the coffee houses in London, while information transmission between London and Newcastle took nine days. Amsterdam and Paris, however, could be reached in two days, due to the simple channel crossing.[31] The description says something about how quickly information about stock developments could reach various places.

The chapter is organised as follows. First, the background of the South Sea and Mississippi Bubbles are described. Second, the development of the economic bubbles and what happened when they burst is discussed; some of the consequences of this development is also discussed. Finally, an analysis is carried out in relation to the perspective argued for here, i.e. innovations lead to economic crises.

Background

Two people in particular are associated with the South Sea Company and the bubble that developed: John Blunt[32] (considered to be the chief architect behind the company) and George Caswall.[33] Blunt had gained considerable experience in the state lottery business; and he used this

---

[30] Mackay (1995: 1–46).
[31] Dale (2004: 4–5).
[32] Sperling (1962: 1–14).
[33] Neale (1990: 91).

expertise to develop his new project.[34] Both Blunt and Caswall were directors in the South Sea Company until the bubble burst in October 1720. In a limited liability company during this period, ordinary people and professional investors could invest in a company without losing more than the face value of the shares they had bought.[35] It may be said that this represented a kind of "democratisation of capitalism", providing opportunities for both the housemaid and the professional investor alike to make investments. This period also saw the publication of books aimed at people other than professional investors, providing investment advice.[36] Around 1690, rich people in England profited from lending money to the government.[37]

A sea captain named Phipps is credited with triggering the new lending ideas for reducing the national debt, which had been accumulated after many long and costly wars. He had made as much as £200,000 for himself and the shareholder investors in his ship, when he recovered great treasures including silver coins from a sunken Spanish galleon off the island of Hispaniola in the West Indies. When this information reached England, dozens of ships set off to the island hoping to make their fortunes in the same way. Diving equipment and deep water divers became sought-after equipment and expertise, respectively. The stock market boomed and many people won and lost fortunes. This episode may be said to characterise the spirit of the age when Blunt was active in business. He was first involved in the development of the Sword Blade Company, whose business was dealing with the government's financial problems. The company bought up large tracts of land in Ireland, and sold these as shares on the stock exchange. The share holders did not receive money as security, but rather part of the national debt (and which today might be described as government bonds). In this way the state could raise funds by selling land in Ireland. The investors had security in that the state paid dividends on the debt, in proportion to the shares they had bought the company, and the government was able to reduce the national debt by

---

[34] Dale (2004: 4).

[35] Paul (2011: 55).

[36] John Houghton's book, *Collection for Improvement of Husbandry and Trade*, was published in 1664; the target audience was people without special expertise in trading (Murphy 2009: 8).

[37] Balen (2003: 31).

raising funds in this way. The investors secured their investments—which ended up in the treasury—by the fact that the state guaranteed payment to investors.

The Sword Blade Company was seen as a competitor to the Bank of England, which had a banking monopoly under a law passed in 1697. The benefits of Blunt's activities to the government were so great that even if they were legally questionable, they became politically possible.

Robert Harley, the Chancellor of the Exchequer, through discussions with John Blunt[38] reached an agreement concerning the establishment of a lottery in 1711 in order to deal with the national debt. People could buy a lottery ticket for £10 and the chance to win a large amount of money when the winning ticket was drawn; however, winnings were not paid out in a lump sum, but in the form of a fixed sum annuity over a period of years (meaning that the government effectively held the prize money as a loan). The money received from the sale of the tickets enabled the government to reduce the national debt. The holders of the tickets had these as a form of security for the amount they had paid, with the added bonus of being able to win an extra-large premium. The success of this was followed by another larger lottery of which the tickets cost £100, with a maximum prize of £20,000![39] This amount was enormous in contemporary terms, as it corresponded to the income of a family from the lower social strata for a period of between 400 and 1333 years.

This incredible opportunity must have created some expectations about the possibility of becoming rich through the financial system, and not just through hard work. Of course, the opportunity only existed for those who were already rich, because the £100 needed to buy a ticket was a large amount of money at the time. Nevertheless, the ingenious part of this scheme was that share dealers could sell shares in the possible winnings, so many of the lower middle class could take part in the expectation of winning unimaginable wealth. Blunt's lottery activities created revenue for the state amounting to about £3.5 million. In other words, many people must have participated in this new "gold mine" (for both

[38] Brian (1988: 20–78).
[39] Balen (2003: 34–35).

the state and those who held winning tickets), perhaps not unlike the current lottery systems in many European countries.

Expectations concerning the additional premium of winnings, as well as the security that all the money would be paid back over time (as it was a loan to the government), may have added fuel to the desire for quick profits and the hope that some stocks would rise sky-high (in relation to the South Sea Bubble that developed a few years later).[40]

Although the lottery activities created great revenues for the state, and winnings for a few lucky lottery ticket holders, the national debt was not paid off, but only deferred to a future date. Everyone who had purchased tickets was entitled to be paid back the face value of their tickets at a later date (the British government was still paying back its lottery ticket debt until 1850).

The next idea that tried to deal with the national debt was the foundation of the South Sea Company on September 10, 1711. The company was granted special privileges by the government, such as a monopoly on the trade with South American colonies, and the authority to used armed force if necessary to ensure effective trading activities.[41] Harley intended to use the company as a new financial instrument (or in the terminology used here, a financial innovation) which ought to be able to compete with the Bank of England and the East India Company. The company was established under the motto: "From Cadiz to the dawn". Harley was elected governor of the company. One third of the company's leadership was politically appointed; five came from Blunt's enterprise the Sword Blade Company.[42] Harley's "propaganda machine" swung into action, and stories about the wonderful possibilities for amassing wealth through the trade in sugar, slaves, cheese, etc. emerged in England. People soon became enthusiastic and wanted to participate in this financial adventure.

The Peace of Utrecht was signed in 1713, and the South Sea Company received its first assignment. The first two vessels transported 2500 slaves to the West Indies, from which the company made a profit of £2500.[43]

---

[40] Paul (2011).
[41] Roseveare (1991).
[42] Balen (2003: 37).
[43] Balen (2003: 41).

From this point on, the company became a "floating financial instrument" whose aim was to deal with the national debt.[44]

The growth of the Mississippi Bubble is associated with the Scottish economist, John Law. His vision of paper money was not well received in Scotland; however, he was able to sell the idea in France. The idea was based on using paper money instead of coins minted from precious metal. He believed that money was only a means of exchanging goods, and did not constitute wealth in itself.[45] In other words, it was the exchange of goods that created value, an idea which was also in line with the Mercantilist thinking of the period.[46]

Law was forced to flee the British Isles, and after a number of years' involvement in financial activities on the continent he was appointed as what today might be called Minister of Finance in France.[47] In 1716 he created a large private bank there, whose share capital consisted of public debt (a type of paper money that may be compared with present-day government bonds). The state guaranteed its value, which increased the level of support and confidence in the new "money". Law's bank began to lend paper money to businessmen, who in turn sold them on. Trade increased and industrial production grew. Eventually, everyone was forced to pay taxes and fees using the "banknotes". Law expanded the idea and issued major credits through his bank, all based on paper money. The money flowed freely and everyone seemed to benefit from this new innovation, the paper money. At the time France did not have institutions such as those which had emerged in Britain: there was no national bank, no large trading company, such as the East India trading company, nor a South Sea Company, which the government could use to sort out its national debt problems. Law used the English national bank as a model when establishing his own private bank; he was also able to use the South Sea Company as a model when organising the Mississippi Company that traded with French colonies in North America, especially along the Mississippi River.[48]

---

[44] Brewer (1989).
[45] John Law is considered as having been responsible for the Mississippi Bubble in 1720.
[46] Magnusson (1994).
[47] "Controller General of Finances of France" under King Louis XV.
[48] Balen (2003: 60–63).

Law's problem was that the paper money that was issued had to comply with the Bank's holdings of gold and silver. The shares in the Mississippi Company became a new way of extending credit and dealing with the national debt; the shares were in a sense a new form of paper money, and they were often exchanged for money. When these shares became interchangeable with money, then the issue of money became in reality detached from gold and silver reserves; and the situation arose where gold and silver in the bank's vaults was no longer the basis for credit. In other words, Law in France, and Blunt in England, had created a new kind of credit system, completely disconnected from banks' holdings of gold and silver. This may be considered to be an institutional innovation.

With the support of the French monarch, Law was able to expand the Mississippi Company and sell shares which were interchangeable with money, and reduce the national debt. In this way, he made himself and many others rich. To provide labour for the French colony, convicts were released from prison and transported to Mississippi; many stories of the forced transportation of criminals and others are described by Balen.[49]

Through his companies Law gradually bought up much of the national debt, so that he emerged as the French state's only official creditor. This special position meant that he was able to gain approval for many of his other projects. Investors in Law's new projects came from all over France, as well as from the Netherlands, England, Germany and Spain.[50] Everyone wanted to "pay homage to the golden calf". With share prices rocketing a building bubble was also growing—new houses were built, and old houses in the towns had an extra floor built on to them. The economy flourished and wealth abounded.[51]

On the other side of the English Canal people were watching with admiration at what was going on. The French national debt could quickly be eliminated if this continued, while the British national debt was not being reduced at the same rate. From 1718 onwards, the ships of the South Sea Company were anchored in harbour due to the conflict with Spain. The South Sea Company—part of the large British national debt

---

[49] Balen (2003: 66–67).
[50] Mackay (1995: 1–45).
[51] Balen (2003: 69).

reduction project—had to be rescued.[52] How long would it take before France managed to rearm and become a military threat to Britain? At least this was the constant refrain of the British authorities.[53] Britain had to do something quickly to rid itself of its national debt, so that France would not pose a future military threat.[54]

Law's economic miracle, however, had a built-in ticking bomb. The issuance of paper money spun out of control, so that it no longer matched any real value, short-term or long-term. The question was—when would the bomb go off? If people panicked and wanted to cash in their paper money and shares with the banks and money lenders, there were not enough coins to pay them. But, no one could see this at the time, in 1719. On the contrary, John Law, through his close relationship to the monarchy, was able to abolish many taxes and financial control mechanisms. This resulted in the food expenses of the poor falling by a third.[55] Everyone believed that the economy was booming. Public buildings were built, the University of Paris was expanded, and new barracks for the soldiers were constructed. All this happened while the shares of the Mississippi Company rose dramatically.[56] Those who had bought early had become rich. It seemed almost too good to be true. In one month in 1719, the share price on the Mississippi Company had risen by 1000 %.[57] Law emerged as France's economic alchemist. However, it was credit that had created money and economic activity. The bomb was still ticking, but no one could hear it. To borrow one's way out of a credit bubble was Law's ingenious invention—a financial innovation that created new money from old loans. Government loans were converted into money by various transactions.[58]

Britain felt directly threatened by the alchemist who managed to get rid of the French national debt, increase revenues in France, re-arm the

---

[52] Paul (2011: 56).

[53] Balen (2003: 68).

[54] Neal (1990: 62–141).

[55] Balen (2003: 70).

[56] Mackay (1995: 1–45).

[57] Balen (2003: 71).

[58] It is not possible over time to borrow one's way out of a credit bubble, but only to save, produce or organise one's way out.

military and threaten the position of the British. Something had to be done!

For Britain, South America, North America and the West Indies were all part of the market of the South Sea Company.[59] Unlimited opportunities for trading, making money and getting rid of the national debt were envisioned, enabling them to compete with France on both the economic and military fronts.

The motivation for the founding South Sea Company was exactly the same as for the Mississippi Company, namely, to refinance the massive national debts that the British and French had acquired during the Spanish War of Succession.[60] In less than ten years, the South Sea Company had created a huge share value of £200 million.[61] The paradox of course was that the company had no income to show for its activities. Whether it was one of the world's greatest scams or just inflated expectations by all parties concerned is hard to say. Possibly the spirit of the times can provide an explanation (including the omnipresent gambling and speculation that characterised the age).[62]

The Bubble

The Growth of the Bubble

Before the advent of limited liability companies, it was not unusual to have shares in single trading voyages; for instance, a voyage to India to purchase spices. The total sum of the parts in the company represented its capital. Any profits were divided in relation to the size of the individual share; losses likewise. Such a venture had a time limit, i.e., the time it took for the ship in question to complete the voyage and transactions. Before limited liability companies were established, it was common for merchants and others to participate in such trading ventures. There

---

[59] Morgan (1928: 143–166); Stein & Stein (2000: 109).

[60] The Spanish Empire was diminished by this war fought between 1701–1714; in its aftermath, the French and the British emerged as the new major powers in Europe.

[61] Dale (2004: 40).

[62] Defoe (2010) (first published in 1719). Defoe was well acquainted with the spirit of the age.

was no market for these shares, i.e., they could not be sold to a third party. With the establishment of limited liability companies, the situation changed completely. More people were now able to purchase shares, and these could be traded in a relatively free market, where the price was determined by supply and demand.[63]

Scott[64] writes that the creation of economic bubbleneeds to have two types of investors, those familiar with the internal dynamics of companies that are subject to speculation, and those who follow in expectation of huge profits. The South Sea Bubble could not have grown without an active market (stock exchange) that could refinance public debt. According to Dale, there were two necessary conditions for the development of the bubble: the stock exchange and the refinancing of the national debt.[65] Lending money to the state was associated with much uncertainty in 1720.[66] Up until 1690, people who lent money to the government in England were given tax concessions. After this period though, lenders could not expect much security for their loans[67]; the government therefore needed to be creative and innovative in order to refinance the national debt.

The public–private loan schemes introduced were new to England and may therefore be considered an innovation, although they had already been used in the Netherlands.[68] The loans were of two kinds: lotteries and bonds. The state paid about 6–10 % interest on loans; whereas, persons with the winning lottery tickets could win relatively large sums of money. About 520,000 lottery tickets valued at £10 each were printed, and later 38,000 lottery tickets valued at £100 each in the period 1711–1714. Between 1693 and 1712, the government managed to raise £10 million on the lottery business. During the same periods, the bonds brought in roughly £11 million.[69] Although these were large amounts, the state still needed to further refinance its national debt.

---

[63] Michie (1999: 16).

[64] Scott (1912), referred to in Neal (1990: 77).

[65] Dale (2004: 22).

[66] The lenders remembered when the king, Charles II, stopped debt payments to creditors in 1672, and had a 50 per cent reduction in the public debt negotiated (Roseveare 1991: 52).

[67] Dickson (1967: 347).

[68] Zaltman et al. (1973).

[69] Dale (2004: 24–25).

In 1714 the British national debt amounted to £48 million, which was astronomical by contemporary standards.[70] Because of the lack of trust, creditors would only lend money based on short-term contracts, which led to the government having constantly to refinance its debt.[71]

It is at this point that the innovation of granting monopolies and privileges to private companies was established. The stock market flourished as a result of these privileges. The difference in the stock market in the 1700s and today was such that the shares were largely traded in what was called "Exchange Alley" in London.[72] This alley was a rumour mill of considerable influence, where true and false information mixed together.[73] Another difference was that there were no long-term institutional investors. Shares traded in the early 1700s were driven by speculation, information in the rumour mill and the desire for short-term super profits.[74] Based on rumours, men and women of different social classes mingled around Exchange Alley in the hope of becoming rich—very rich and very quickly.[75] Then, as now, future contracts ("futures") were entered into options on the purchases and sales at certain rates and certain dates.[76]

The South Sea Bubble and the Mississippi Bubble appear to be linked in time and through the innovative financial instruments that were developed in both countries. The correlation of price movements on the stock exchanges of Amsterdam, London and Paris in 1719–1720 show that there was a close connection between the three exchanges. Throughout 1719, the share prices of the three exchanges were relatively constant. In January 1720, the first incidents occur that indicate that something is about to happen. The share prices rise sharply, but then fall to a "normal" level. From April to October 1720, share prices explode on the three exchanges.[77] In this way, one can say that the South Sea Bubble and the

---

[70] Roseveare (1991: 52).

[71] Dickson (1967: 39–40).

[72] Exchange Alley is a narrow alleyway that is bounded by Lombard Street, Cornhill and Birchin Lane.

[73] Defoe 2010 (first published in 1719).

[74] Francis 2011 (first published in 1849).

[75] Defoe (2010).

[76] Dale (2004: 37).

[77] Neal (1990: 65).

Mississippi Bubble were the first international economic share bubbles in history.[78] In December 1720, the bubble burst.

It seems, however, some people must have known about the implications of the growth of the bubble, because during the same period as share prices rise, the price of gold on the London Stock Exchange also increased greatly and far above the normal price.[79] If we compare this trend in gold with the advice of Hoare's Bank, then this rise in the price of gold makes sense.[80]

In the spring of 1719, the bubble began to grow on the Paris stock exchange.[81] No one, however, at that time could see that this was happening, as it is always difficult to determine when a bubble actually starts to develop. An initial change in share values is often seen only as "background noise" by investors. Money flowed in, however, on a large scale from London to Paris to participate in the profit opportunities that John Law had laid the groundwork for.[82]

At the end of 1719 in Paris, and in the first two months of 1720, it was no longer possible to cash in on super profits that were possible before these dates. This is indicated by the number of investors who sold out of the Paris Stock Exchange and invested on the London Stock Exchange.[83] The shares of the Mississippi Company fell sharply in February 1720. Meanwhile the British Parliament approved the South Sea Company's plan to take over large parts of the British national debt. This led to a further flight of capital from Paris to the London stock exchange.[84] On 23 February, Law managed through financial dexterity to get the shares of the Mississippi Company to rise again, but volatility was very high. It

---

[78] The Tulip Bubble in 1637 was not an international phenomenon in the same sense as the South Sea Bubble and the Mississippi Bubble in 1720.

[79] The normal price ranged from £3.88 to £3.92 per ounce, while from July to November 1920 it rose to £4.08 (Neal 1990: 65–66).

[80] Gold prices are very volatile. This can be explained by the fact that one sells gold when the prices of shares continue to rise, but take safeguarding measures shortly afterwards by buying gold. When share prices continue to rise, one will participate in the rally and sell gold. One dare not remain too long in the stock market, because it is assumed there may be a bubble, and so one safeguards oneself again by buying gold. The volatility in gold may be called the "Ashton Effect" due to the fact that T.S. Ashton first discovered volatility in exchange rates during economic crises (Ashton 1969: 113).

[81] Carswell (1993: 101).

[82] Neal (1990: 68).

[83] Scott (1912, Vol. 1: 404).

[84] Neal (1990: 69).

seems the road towards the end had begun, and from June to September 1720 the Mississippi Bubble burst.[85]

According to Neal's statistical analyses,[86] the South Sea Bubble grew between February 23 and June 15, 1720; it was also during this period that money poured into the London Stock Exchange from the other exchanges in Europe, especially from Amsterdam. In the same way English and Irish investors played a major role in the development of the Mississippi Bubble, the Dutch investors played an important role in the growth of the South Sea Bubble.[87] As mentioned above, the Mississippi Bubble burst before the South Sea Bubble, resulting in money flowing from the Paris Stock Exchange to the London Stock Exchange, which led to pressure on the South Sea Bubble; in other words, this may be said to have been a type of financial contagion.

From April to August 1720, stocks rose sharply in the South Sea Company. However, it was not only this company that increased its share value. Most of the shares on the London Stock Exchange rose sharply, among others, various insurance companies, although they did not rise as much as the South Sea Company.[88] In an effort to prevent increasing competition for investors, the leadership of the company used its influence in the government to pass the Bubble Act (June 1720), which in reality prohibited the founding of companies without government recognition.[89] What triggered the bubble to burst is discussed by several writers; Harris claims that the Act was not a surprise to the market, and that it is therefore unlikely that it triggered the bubble to burst.[90]

The Bubble Bursts

After August 18, 1720, the share value of the South Sea Company started to fall.[91] Information quickly moved across the channel, and shareholder

---

[85] Carswell (1993: 136; 165–166).
[86] Neal (1990, 77; 80–88).
[87] Dickson (1967: 123–143).
[88] Paul (2011: 48).
[89] Supple (1970: 26–28).
[90] Harris (1994: 610–627).
[91] Goldgar (2007: 306).

value in Dutch companies also began to fall in October.[92] The South Sea Bubble burst in autumn 1720. Many lost huge sums. Some, however, had borrowed most of what they had invested in shares, and they lost everything they owned.

The fear was that the entire economy of Britain would break down as a result of the burst bubble. Questions were asked in the British Parliament about how this was possible, and investigations were initiated.[93] The only results that came out of these investigations were that it involved fraud and a speculative mania that developed in the stock market.[94] The answer, though, could be a simple one. Perhaps some major investors saw that stock was greatly over-valued, and began to sell out in order to consolidate profits and prevent large losses. There may be an even simpler answer. Perhaps some major investors needed cash, and sold out in order to increase their cash reserves. It may also be the case that some key investors saw better opportunities elsewhere, such as in the Netherlands and Germany,[95] and thus started selling out of the South Sea Company. Increased competition may also have put pressure on share prices.[96] Bad news for the shipping industry, such as reports of the plague in Marseilles in July 1720 could have caused a shock amongst investors triggering the sale.[97] A simple thing such as the fact that many of the farmers who had invested in the South Sea Company needed money in August 1720 in order to pay agricultural workers may also have triggered the crash.[98] Carswell writes that Sir John Blunt even bought a lot of shares in August and September to increase share value further.[99] This may have caused some key investors to cash in their profits.

The Mississippi Bubble burst in 1720. It is reasonable to assume that investors in the South Sea Company tried to consolidate their profits by

---

[92] Dickson (1967: 140–141; 152).

[93] Paul (2011: 43).

[94] Balen (2003: 95–129).

[95] Carswell (2001: 136) and Dickson (1967: 152) suggest this possibility concerning what triggered the bubble to burst.

[96] Dickson (1967: 145).

[97] Carswell (2001: 166).

[98] Ashton (1969).

[99] Carswell (2001: 140). Dickson (1967: 142) says that the assumption is difficult to prove.

starting to sell out of the South Sea Company, when they knew that John Law had also based his actions precisely in the "South Sea".[100] Both Paris and London stock exchanges experienced that investors bought shares and then quickly sold them again. The aim was to make profits.[101]

All these factors may have triggered the avalanche, which, however, was there, ready to fall. When an avalanche develops, then anyone who has seen one knows that almost any small factor can trigger it. In September 1720, the Sword Blade Bank experienced financial difficulties and went bankrupt.

The whole of the British national debt had been converted into shares and bonds in the South Sea Company, the East India Company and the Bank of England. The Bank of England, who had agreements with the South Sea Company concerning the sale of shares at a certain price, withdrew from the agreement, which increased the downturn for the company.[102]

From a peak value of £1000 per share, the price fell to £124 in December 1720. Everyone was now aware of the fact that the bubble had burst.[103] Consequences, scapegoats and explanations were now on the political agenda.

Analysis

The London Stock Exchange: An Institutional Innovation

The growth of financial capitalism, i.e. where one could freely buy and sell shares on a stock exchange, is an institutional innovation that came into existence with the establishment of the Amsterdam Stock Exchange in the early 1600s. In the case of England, this occurred with the estab-

---

[100] Murphy (1997).
[101] Paul (2011: 50).
[102] Dickson (1967: 166).
[103] Neal (1990: 90–96).

lishment of the London Stock Exchange in 1698. The concept of financial capitalism first emerged in the late 1800s.[104]

The person who is associated with the transfer of the Dutch financial system to England is the Bishop of Salisbury, Gilbert Burnet.[105] After a period of time, the financial system in the Netherlands and England spread throughout Europe. It is reasonable to assume that this institutional innovation started the development of financial capitalism in Europe.[106]

My argument here, which is consistent with the cliometric school,[107] is that what happened on the stock exchanges in England, the Netherlands and France was essentially rational behaviour, and not driven by a type of "mania". We know today that stock speculation was characterised by a type of mania, but what drove prices up was a rational action to make a profit. In other words, as long as it is not wrong to want to make money, often a lot of money, then it seems reasonable to assume that trading on the stock market when share prices rise characterises rational behaviour. To act as shares plunge is an expression of a strong belief in the future, insider information, or expectations of future price falls and "future" purchases. Although many lost money in the South Sea Bubble, we have also seen that many made huge profits. Is it irrational to make investments to reap profits? Or is it irrational to invest and lose, when the risk of loss is always present in the stock market? It seems reasonable to assume that the stock market in the new exchanges was involved in the growth of the bubble. It was not that some people became infected with behavioural mania, and acted like sheep in a flock that was the starting point of the bubble. Investors purchase of shares on the new exchanges was on the whole largely rational, i.e., in the sense that it is rational to desire to make a profit.

---

[104] Neal (1990: 4).

[105] Dickson (1967: 17).

[106] Dickson (1967: 311–312).

[107] It must, however, be pointed out that the cliometric school even although it may use the world's finest and complex mathematics and computers to compare the data, the patterns cannot be used to explain why these patterns occur. It is the explanation of the emergence of these patterns that the relationship between different types of innovations and economic crises can provide.

As mentioned above, the stock market was organised in England about 1698, around the coffee houses in Exchange Alley, London.[108] In this context, it is important to understand that an institutional innovation, a regulation concerning stocks, was necessary in order to promote trading in shares. The reason is that historically shares couldn't be acquired by another in principle, but followed the person who had entered into an agreement, a form of shared property with restrictions one might say. Such stocks or shares were difficult to sell. It was only when limited companies had sections written into their foundation charters that share trading developed in Exchange Alley.[109] In this way the shares became more marketable than the other documents in Exchange Alley. The capital market in London adapted to these changes.[110] The shares were perceived as an innovation and were more liquid than bonds, lottery tickets and "tallies".[111]

Options, "Futures" and Government Lottery Activities: Economic and financial Innovations

The financial innovations in England have their roots in 1693 and 1694. First it was the fixed interest rate on government bonds in 1693 that was not an immediate success. Then came the state lotteries in 1694, which were a little more successful.[112] The first overview of the financial instruments that were used on the stock exchange was published in the Netherlands in 1688 in De la Vega's work, *Confusion de Confusiones*.[113] The financial innovations thus started in the late 1600s. England was at war and had just gone through a revolution (The Glorious Revolution of 1688), which obviously had a great impact on people's daily lives; more

---

[108] Carruthers (1996: 170).

[109] Jones (1978: 285).

[110] Neal (1990: 90).

[111] Paul (2011: 32). "Tallies" were originally wooden sticks which were in two parts, where the creditor had the one part and the debtor other. Later, these two parts settled in paper notes that together showed who owed what to whom (Paul 2011: 130, note 20).

[112] Neal (1990: 14).

[113] De la Vega 1957 (English translation) (first edition in 1688 in Spanish)

so than financial innovations, such as the stock market and the financial innovations that followed in its wake, which only affected a minority.

Innovations in the context of financial instruments are often referred to in the literature on the subject as the English financial revolution.[114] Roseveare[115] writes that this revolution is about the creation of the Bank of England, the national debt system and the emergence of the first signs of a British stock market. There has been discussion about what caused the English financial revolution. One can say that two schools of thought stand out here. One school focuses on the demand side, where war and war debts are the main factors. The other school is focused on the supply side, and considers the new institutional innovations as the main instruments of the financial revolution.[116] A real innovation in relation to the financial instruments was the public lotteries. The largest financial innovation was however the possibility of trading in shares.

Public: Private Loan Schemes: Institutional Innovation

The ideas of the new public–private loan schemes came from the Netherlands, where their banking system made it possible for the Dutch to trade internationally, have colonies in Asia and carry out military activities around the world.[117] These loan schemes had existed in the Netherlands since the Tulip Bubble in 1637.[118]

The financial system in the Netherlands, which was transferred to England, was based on public–private lending schemes, in which the state paid annual interest rates for loans that were made in the market. In this way they could compete for loans and get the lowest possible rates on bonds. The bonds were of two types. The government could redeem the first type of bond, whereas, the second type could not be redeemed before

---

[114] Paul (2011: 31).

[115] Roseveare (1991)

[116] Carruthers (1996: 116–121).

[117] Brewer (1989: 24).

[118] Goldgar (2007). Public–private projects were, however, already in existence in the second century in the Roman Empire, especially in connection with the mining industry, for instance in Spain.

the date fixed. The government could redeem the first type of bond when interest rates were low, so refinancing could take place at a lower interest rate. The second type of bond was at fixed rates that lasted a number of years.[119] The latter were often held by private companies, such as the South Sea Company. The bonds were exchanged for shares in, amongst others, the South Sea Company. It was the expectations concerning a company's future business that made the public investments interesting. This is also where both John Law in France and John Blunt in England used the world's first economic spin to promote expectations and increase the likelihood of public investments in private companies.

The English Revolution, 1688, and the Peace of Utrecht, 1713: Institutional Innovations

After the English Revolution in 1688, British finances gradually changed. What was really new in relation to the English Revolution, from an innovation perspective, was a change in attitude towards the capital market. One viewed the stock market, which had existed in Exchange Alley for some time already, as a new phenomenon. People became aware of the market and began to invest there.[120] A brand new financial system based on, amongst other things, a large-scale use of foreign loan agreements, which could be redeemed in shares of companies such as the South Sea Company, took over the national debt.

Paper Money: Borrowing Your Way Out of a Credit Bubble: An Economic, Financial Innovation

Paper money instead of coins containing gold and silver was first introduced in France by John Law. After the introduction of this innovation people could visit a bank and change their bank notes into coins. However, by May 1720 the banks had issued so many bank notes that they were twice as many bank notes as they had coins available, which

---

[119] Carruthers (1996: 75–76).
[120] Dickson (1967: 486).

led to a tremendous inflationary pressure in France. One result of this pressure was that bank notes were devalued to half their face value.[121] The devaluation of bank notes was carried out on 21 May 1720. The confidence in the new monetary system involving bank notes broke down. British diplomats in Paris reported that people felt they had been robbed by the state for half of what they owned.[122] The revolts in the streets of Paris led to the decision of 21 May being withdrawn. Nevertheless, confidence in the new monetary system was shattered. On May 29, John Law was put under house arrest.[123] From this point on John Law was no longer the leader of the Mississippi Company, and it was put under state control. The right to redeem bank notes was suspended between June and October 1720. Confidence in the new money system was now very low. The exchange rate on bank notes was changed five times during a short period of time, and confidence in bank notes broke down completely.

From 27 November 1720, there were no banks that exchanged bank notes into coins.[124]

The attempt to borrow their way out of a credit bubble by introducing new means of payment, bank notes, was not the success that John Law had aimed at.

What happened in summer 1720 was that people lost confidence in stocks, bank notes and the authorities handling of the value of bank notes, because these were devalued several times. People's confidence in the Mississippi Company was reflected in the drastic fall in share prices. In January 1720, the shares stood at £325, while in September the same year they had fallen to £50. The fall of 80 % corresponded with the fall of the shares in the South Sea Company between July and December 1720.[125] Both France and Britain had attempted to borrow their way out of a credit crisis by creating new monetary innovations and institutions that would implement these innovations.[126] The result was loss of confidence in the system and many people lost everything they owned.

---

[121] Dale (2004: 127).

[122] Murphy (1997: 250).

[123] Dale (2004: 128).

[124] Murphy (1997: 283).

[125] Dale (2004: 131).

[126] Both countries had taken up large loans during the War of the Spanish Succession. Paper money was the innovation that would bring down the national debt by converting the debt to the bank

The entire financial system of France was discredited. This lack of confidence spread over the English Channel, and was one of the precipitating causes of the serious trouble the South Sea Company found itself in, i.e., people's distrust of the stock value of the company.

When the Mississippi Bubble burst,[127] it had a twofold effect on the development of the South Sea Bubble. The immediate effect was that several investors flocked from Paris to London. They helped to increase the value of the shares in the South Sea Company, through increased demand. Gradually, people began to compare trends in the Mississippi Company with the South Sea Company, resulting in people starting to sell out.[128]

Mercantilism's Breakthrough in Europe

Mercantilist doctrine dominated European economic thinking in the 1600–1700s; it was replaced by economic liberalism in the 1800s as the main model.[129]

Mercantilism, which views trade as being the main cause of economic prosperity, came to expression in two ways. First, trade was considered to be the main driving force for value creation in a country. Therefore, trading companies should be granted monopolies, privileges and be protected by the use of military force. Second, mercantilism was a way of understanding the economic system, where equilibrium and economic self-regulation were focused upon.[130] The main principle of the doctrine is represented by the first element, where commerce, government and military resources are interwoven, as we saw to be the case in the South Sea and Mississippi companies; another aspect of the main principle was that the larger the trade surplus a country had, the richer the country was. This thinking, which reigned in Europe in 1500 well into the 1700s,

---

notes guaranteed by the government and banks. The instruments used in the two countries were respectively the Mississippi Company and the South Sea Company.

[127] The Mississippi Bubble burst in summer, 1720.

[128] Dale (2004: 131).

[129] Magnusson (1994).

[130] Gramp (1952: 466).

promoted colonial expansion. To protect home production and increase exports, many toll barriers were introduced to hinder imports. Tariffs were placed specifically on finished goods in contrast to raw materials in order to bolster domestic production. Other consequences of the mercantilist doctrine were the following: monopolisation; silver and gold became the main expression of a country's wealth; laws preventing the use of a country's ships to transport the goods of other countries (the Navigation Acts), as well as export subsidies, to name a few.[131] The principal Mercantilist ideas[132] are best demonstrated by contrasting them to that which superseded the Mercantilist doctrine, the ideas of Adam Smith and the Physiocrats. While Smith focused on free trade and the Physiocrats focused on agricultural production, Mercantilist doctrine was most concerned with government control and protectionist measures.[133] In other words, a political, economic idea had consequences for a country's economy, for instance, the development of both the Mississippi and South Sea Bubbles.

Reflection

In 1719–1720, the stock exchange in Exchange Alley in London was affected by the events in France, where John Law had developed something similar to what John Blunt had created in England. Hutcheson's analysis[134] of the South Sea bubble, which was written just after the bubble burst, provides the only contemporary attempt to explain the bubble. The other contemporary observers who wrote about the phenomenon restricted themselves mainly to "mania" descriptions.[135]

Some writers use cliometric research[136] to explain the growth and bursting of the bubble. This research is based on mathematics. It must

---

[131] Hutchinson (1978: 23).

[132] It has been questioned whether Mercantilist doctrine was an overall coherent system of thought (Magnusson 1994: 21–60).

[133] However, not all Mercantilists argued for protectionist measures (Magnusson 1994: 8).

[134] Hutcheson 2010 (first published in 1721)

[135] Paul (2011: 75).

[136] Neal (1990); Paul (2011).

be stressed, however, that although mathematics is used as a basis for cliometric research, it is nevertheless not a theory that addresses the reasons for the growth of the bubble. It is only a description and analysis of share price patterns once the first indications of a bubble have become evident, until the "point of no return" shows up in the statistical material. Cliometric research can make an important contribution to understanding how stock prices evolve into a bubble, and while the bubble lasts. However, it cannot help us to answer the question of why a bubble occurs. It is the last question that I have focused on here, as illustrated in Fig. 4.1.

In the South Sea bubble, as with other bubbles, as long as everything was going well, and everyone was making money on the rising share prices, there was no investigation concerning share price developments in the South Sea Company. It was only when more and more people lost their money as the share price fell that cries of "bribery" and "trickery" were to be heard.

Research into the South Sea Bubble may be divided into three approaches. One approach is represented here in this chapter, as well as partly by Neal.[137] This approach attempts to demonstrate that innovation leads to economic crises. Another approach proposes that the South Sea Bubble was the result of mania, trickery and the gambling tendencies[138] that were characteristic of the age. The third approach uses cliometric research and financial instruments to prove that there was no mania, although there were aspects of trickery and bribery.[139]

The cliometric research and innovation approaches argue that the bubble was mainly the result of rational motives.[140] Kindelberger, former Professor of Economics at MIT, explains that individual behaviour is often rational, but that the sum of rational actions may result in irrational

---

[137] Neal (1990).

[138] Hutcheson (2010); (2010a); Dickson (1967); Carswell (1993, 2001); Scott (1912).

[139] Paul (2011); Neal (1990); Kindelberger (1996); Garber (2000). One of Garber's points is that bribery was an integral part of decision-making at the time, and says nothing about the trickery concerning share prices being planned (Garber 2000: 111). It was not irrational to invest in a stock that rose; on the contrary, it was rational (Garber 2000: 125). One of Garber's points is precisely that if something went wrong, it does not mean it was wrong in principle.

[140] Rational bubbles are stressed by Garber (2000).

behaviour. He argues that small discrepancies at the beginning of a process can lead to serious negative consequences later on.[141] He may be said to be using chaos theory in this context, or, more specifically, the "butterfly effect" in chaos theory.[142]

My criticism of cliometric research is not that it is erroneous, but that the analysis does not explain anything about the origin of economic bubbles. It only describes what happens, and then uses the pattern of what is happening to say something about similar conditions in share prices at a later date. It would be the same as calculating that the tides occur twice a day with a negative time lag of one hour. Such an insight may obviously have some practical uses, but it would say nothing about why the ocean has tidal movements. In order to see this it is necessary to step outside the system in focus. The same also applies when explaining economic bubbles. One must go beyond the bubbles and expand the system boundaries to discover explanations that are relevant to the specific calculations which, amongst others, cliometric research is concerned with.

Figure 4.1 shows the relationship between innovation, social mechanisms and the South Sea Bubble. Much of what has been written about the South Sea Bubble can also be applied to the Mississippi Bubble.

---

[141] Kindleberger (1996: 23).

[142] The point of chaos theory is that the system is so interconnected that small changes in one place can have a big impact somewhere else in the system due to various multiplier effects. The butterfly effect is meant to illustrate this by saying that if a butterfly flaps its wings in China, this can later cause a storm in Greenland. Obviously, this is only intended as a figurative image for network effects in an interconnected system.

Innovation	Social mechanisms	Phenomena

London Stock Exchange (1698)
(institutional innovation)

Options, lottery og "futures"
(economic, financial innovation)

New public-private loan schemes
(institutional innovation)

New paper money
(economic, financial innovation)

The English Revolution in 1688
and the Peace of Utrecht 1713
(institutional innovation)

The world's first PR -spin
(economic innovation)

Mercantilism dominates
European economic thinking
(institutional innovation)

Great speculations

Complexity and the systematic
risk increases

Many competing for the
the same resources

Increased trading on the
stock exchange

People's relation to money
and security is positively
changed

Resulted in a great increase in
share prices

Trade becomes the most
Important force in value creation

triggers

triggers

reinforces

South Sea Bubble
1720

reinforces

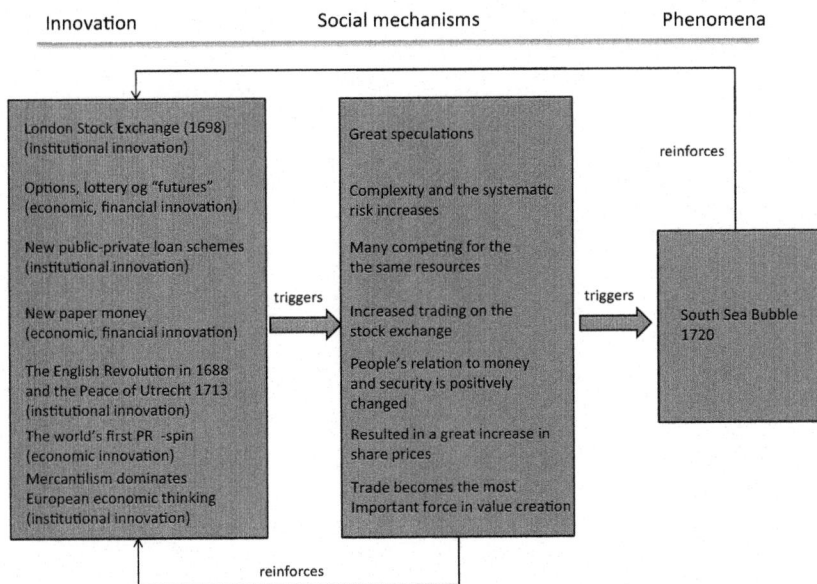

Fig. 4.1 The South sea bubble of 1720

5

The Long Depression: 1873–1893

Introduction

Industrial innovations are not synonymous with the Industrial Revolution. The Industrial Revolution began in Britain in the 1750s and spread via different routes to the rest of Europe and the USA. Industrial innovations, on the other hand, are a more continuous phenomenon.[1] The nascent industrial era caused changes in production, distribution, consumption, productivity and ways of thinking. This period saw the emergence of a whole new class of industrial workers who were disciplined through the new industrial organisation of work, such as on assembly lines and in factory hierarchies.

Industrialisation and modernity went hand in hand. This led, among other things, to new institutions in most Western countries.[2] Status, position and power changed hands. Production in the towns and cities presupposed distribution of goods to consumers who lived and worked in these urban centres. This was one reason for the substantial railway

---

[1] Landes (2003: 1).
[2] Landes (2003: 6).

© The Author(s) 2017
J.-A. Johannessen, *Innovations Lead to Economic Crises*,
DOI 10.1007/978-3-319-41793-6_5

construction during this period.[3] Merchants and industrialists gradually took over the power and position of the rural aristocracy.

Hoffman[4] based his analysis of the crisis of the late 1800s on Keynesian input–output analysis.[5] Newer historical findings are used to complement Hoffmann's analysis.[6]

The period 1873–1897 may be viewed as constituting a continual economic crisis. The crisis was "global", but emerged in different ways in different countries. In Britain, for example, the economic crisis primarily affected the middle classes. In the rest of Europe and the USA, the majority of the population was affected. At the time, the economic crisis was termed "the Great Depression". Although the economic crisis affected many people, it was also a time when many new companies were founded and became economically established. Viewed in a broader perspective, the economic crisis marked a transition from an early British industrialisation phase to a new era of industrialisation. One of the results was that large parts of Europe and the USA also went through an industrialisation process.

Between 1850 and 1873 there had been a strong economic growth in Europe and the USA. This was mainly caused by the fact that areas outside of Britain were drawn into industrial development. This particularly applied to agriculture in these areas. Improved agricultural production resulted in an influx of cheap labour to industrial areas from rural areas, and the production of agricultural machinery increased agricultural production.[7] This development led to the demand for railroads and steam ships to transport raw materials to factories and finished goods to markets. The economic growth in continental Europe and in the USA also stimulated economic growth in Britain.

---

[3] Taylor (1951).

[4] Hoffmann 1970 (first published in 1955).

[5] In 1973, Wassily Leontief received the Nobel Prize in economics for developing input-output theory.

[6] The criticism of Hoffmann's analysis is that the data used for input-output analyses is poor. Hoffmann in the preface to the latest edition has complemented the data with a fifty-page preface.

[7] Hobsbawn (1968: 103–104).

The new machinery and transport systems meant that productivity rose and costs were reduced. Thus, prices for goods also dropped, and the pressure to reduce wages followed. The consequence was 20 years of deflation, where prices of goods, services and wages were reduced. These conditions were called "the Great Depression" [8] at the time. It was the agricultural sector that was affected the most. Reductions in the prices of agricultural products resulted in a poorer economic situation for the individual farmer.

When the cheap goods reached the European market around 1870, the bottom fell out of agricultural production, Hobsbawn notes.[9] This phenomenon spread to the USA, whose exports depended on out-competing European agricultural products on price. One of the results of this was that many countries protected their agricultural production by imposing tariffs on imported goods. The protectionist measures, however, were first introduced around 1879 after the crisis had rumbled on for a good number of years; this meant that the crisis was prolonged by political means. For, paradoxically, although the protectionist measures improved conditions in the short term, they prolonged the crisis, because they prevented trade between countries, which hampered economic growth and thus the resolution of the crisis.

The innovations that had led to progress and economic growth in Britain during the first industrial phase were the same innovations that strangled the economy and brought about an economic crisis in the country: innovations led not only to increased productivity but also to a reduction in costs, prices and wages. However, in the longer term, it was precisely these innovations that transformed the economy and led to economic growth; but it took 20 years before this growth set in.

For Britain, which had a developed industry by contemporary standards, the reduction in the price of imported agricultural products was considered to be a clear advantage. The reduction in the price of agricultural goods led to further pressure to mechanise and increase agricultural productivity in Britain. As mentioned, this led to a surplus of rural workers who moved to urban areas to work in the factories.

---

[8] Hobsbawn (1968: 105).
[9] Hobsbawn (1968: 105).

Many people in the British middle and upper classes had invested in industrialisation, for instance, in railway construction in the USA and the Ottoman Empire. When these areas began to be affected by the crisis, the large profits to be made through investment also dried up. On the other hand, the poor in Britain did not suffer directly as a result of the Great Depression, because there was work, although the pay was low. It was the middle and upper classes who were mainly affected by the crisis in Britain, because the areas where they had invested their money were affected by the crisis.

The crisis resulted in France, Germany and the USA protecting themselves by erecting tariff barriers against the import of cheap agricultural goods from Britain and the British colonies. Eventually these were applied to manufactured goods from Britain as well, in order to build up their domestic industries.[10] Britain, which was more industrially advanced and needed to trade worldwide, argued for free trade, whereas the other countries argued for protectionist policies.

One of the consequences of the "Great Depression" was that Britain lost its monopoly in two areas: industrialisation and imperialism. From the 1880s onwards, several of the major European powers made imperialist gains in Africa and Asia. Probably the most important consequence of the Great Depression was that the new industrial powers were able to compete with Britain. There is much to suggest that a closer alliance between private capital and the state was another result of the crisis.[11]

The economic crisis led to the rise of the labour movement in Britain. Great changes in the 1850s led to new ideas concerning the unity of the working class. Political parties on the left side of the political scale, including Marxist political parties, were founded after the Great Depression. It is reasonable to assume that the industrial and political wings of the labour movement grew out of the Great Depression as a social reaction to the economic crisis. Here, prospect theory offers an explanation of why this could happen.[12]

---

[10] Hobsbawn (1968: 107).

[11] Hobsbawn (1968: 108).

[12] Johannessen (2014a) (IJIM - forthcoming). Prospect theory is used to explain the relationship between innovation and economic crises.

The chapter is organised as follows. First, the theoretical rationale for the relationship between innovations and economic crises is reviewed. Second, the background of the crisis in Britain and the rest of Europe and the USA is described and discussed. Third, relevant developments before the crisis are briefly considered. Fourth, the actual crisis is examined. Finally, the crisis on the basis of the selected perspective here, which is that innovations lead to economic crises, is analysed.

Background

Britain

Hobsbawn calls the period from 1840 to 1895 the "the Second Phase of Industrialisation".[13] The industrialisation of the textile industry had been completed and new industrial projects were knocking on the door. The period is characterised by the introduction of the electric telegraph and railroad construction.[14] The revolution in the means of transport through the introduction of the railways and steam-powered ships resulted in an increased demand for coal, iron and steel[15]: these commodities also linked industrialisation to the rest of Europe and the USA. The economy in Britain and the rest of Europe flourished between 1830 and 1873. Textile exports increased in value but dropped as a percentage of total British exports, because of the increase in the export of coal, iron and steel, and machinery.[16] The 1842 repeal on the ban on exports of industrial machinery in the textile industry is an indication that British industry felt secure enough in its position to export such products to the rest of Europe.

The second phase of industrialisation was characterised by strong industrial growth that encompassed most European countries and the USA.[17]

---

[13] Hobsbawn (1968: 88).
[14] Hobsbawn (1968: 88).
[15] Landes (2003: 90–100).
[16] Hobsbawn (1968: 89).
[17] For Europe see Landes (2003: 90–100; For USA see Hoffmann 1970: 3–9).

Labour productivity increased greatly due to the considerable mechanisation of manual work. For instance, in the forges, the brawny arms of the smith were replaced by the steam hammer. In the textile industry, many textile workers were replaced by machines and made redundant. The demand for iron and steel exploded, in part due to the increase in the production of new machinery. The machines were often steam-powered and required coal to fire them, whereas before they had been dependent on wood to fuel them or water power. Canal transport had depended on horses, which were now largely replaced by steam-powered engines; for instance, five hundred horses could be replaced by a single locomotive (hence the name "Iron Horse"). Coal and steam also transformed society in other ways. Sailing ships were replaced by steam-powered vessels over a period of time. This obviously led to movement in the labour force; for instance, redundant sail makers would generally seek employment in factories in urban areas. Urban development was the result of the first industrial phase between 1750 and 1840.[18] The widespread use of coal, iron, steel and steam meant that the second phase of industrialisation affected society in very different ways than it had in the first industrial phase: coal, iron, steel and steam integrated the various areas in the first phase of industrialisation, and the first phase of industrialisation also penetrated social structures. Industry became the driving force of economic growth; agriculture became less important, but was still vital in that it needed to feed a growing industrial population.

During the second industrialisation phase, industrial modes of production, new transportation and the consumption of finished goods spread throughout Europe. In addition to iron, steel, coal and steam power, new knowledge was also developed during the second phase. Chemical expertise and the chemical industries were an important part of the second phase.[19] The chemical industry had slowly evolved from the first industrial phase using various bleaching agents.[20] What is new in this context

---

[18] Hobsbawn (1968: 88) places the second phase of the industrial revolution in the period 1840–1895.

[19] Landes (2003: 108).

[20] Various forms of alkali were used. Before the development of the chemical industry forests were cut down so that soda could be extracted from the ashes of the burnt wood. This bottleneck in

is that new knowledge created a new branch of industry, the chemical industry.

It was the shift in the relative importance of the various factors of production, such as iron, steel, coal, steam and chemicals, that led to the second industrial phase. In this phase society, organisations, knowledge and employment conditions were transformed.

Already by the 1830s, hundreds of thousands of men, women and children were employed in factories. From a Marxist perspective, the industrial proletariat was created during this period. Landes[21] makes an interesting point when he argues that the increasing cost of labour, strikes or the threat of strikes led to an increasing mechanisation. In today's terminology, one could say that higher wages increase productivity because of the incentive to reduce labour costs. Landes explains the relationship between wages, productivity and innovation during this period as follows: "In sum, high wages were a stimulus to innovation and technological advance."[22] When the cost of labour rose, without concomitant productivity increases, then this led, amongst other things, to yarn being shipped from Britain to Central Europe to be woven into cloth, because labour was cheaper there. From the mid-1850s, however, the supply of labour in England increased for a number of reasons, including the mechanisation of agriculture. Another reason for the increased supply of cheap labour was the influx of cheap labour from Ireland and Scotland. In addition, women and children provided cheap labour for the textile industry. This meant that much of the production remained in England.

The second industrial phase was to a large degree about competition for labour costs, focus on standardisation, mass production and quality. This resulted in increased specialisation within and between countries. Specialisation also led to technological innovations that increased productivity and promoted competitiveness. This in turn provided the basis for higher wages and an increasing domestic demand for goods and

---

production was removed due to processes used in the chemical industry in the late 1860s, although the expertise stems from around 1823 (Landes 2003: 110).

[21] Landes (2003: 114).

[22] Landes (2003: 116).

services in Britain and the other countries that were industrialised.[23] The tendency was towards industrialisation, urbanisation and specialisation of the labour force. This development led to new jobs and the need for new educational forms and paths of education, such as in banking, butchery, carpentry, plumbing, etc.

It was the institutional and economic innovations that enabled this development. The economic innovations were mainly material innovations: new production processes, products and raw materials characterised development, which led to capital flowing to those areas where the potential for profit was greatest. Capital became oriented towards and concentrated on "technological production". Landes writes about this development: "The factory was a new bridge between invention and innovation".[24] Capital made innovations possible while the new capital flowed to innovative businesses. What came first, innovation or capital in this context is not so interesting; what's interesting is that capital accumulated around innovations. The fact that capital became concentrated around technological innovations in the factories also meant that the shares of these companies became attractive. Although several economic historians argue that industry was of no importance in the overall economic statistics,[25] it was this part of the economy that capital and innovations flowed to. However, the economy was only moments away from crisis, if something were to go wrong.

Eventually, agriculture, financial institutions, transport and trade became dependent on production and innovation in the factories. It is reasonable to assume that when the entire economic system is connected in a new way, with factories as a driving force, an industrial revolution and institutional innovation have taken place. This seems to have occurred sometime between 1850 and 1873.

Innovations led the market out of equilibrium, and innovations were perceived to be continuous. The middle and upper classes felt that they lived in the best of all worlds, writes Landes.[26] Investment in factory production, the new technological innovations, the railways and chemical

---

[23] Landes (2003: 117–119).
[24] Landes (2003: 122).
[25] Landes (2003: 122).
[26] Landes (2003: 122–123).

production continued. Capital was concentrated around the innovations, where the opportunity for profit was great, but where the risk of loss was also great.

The Liverpool—Manchester line (1830) gave a return of 10 % on invested capital.[27] This meant that capital flowed to railway construction around other cities, because the expectation of large returns was high. As yields fell, interest rates came in line with public stock at around 3–4 %.

The transport system was based on steam power, first rail transport and then steamships. However, it was not until the 1880s that the tonnage of steamships exceeded that of sail in Britain.[28]

From 1850 to 1880, the production of iron, steel and coal was formidable in Britain. While iron and coal production was based on established technology, there were three innovations in steel production in 1850, 1860s and 1870s.[29] The main result of these innovations was that steel could be mass produced, resulting in a dramatic increase in production. This affected the construction of railways, steamships, etc. Growth in productivity also affected profitability and wages positively. At the same time, labour could be used to increase the production of railways and steamships. In addition, increased agricultural productivity led to improved profitability freeing labour that could be transferred to industry. The following example illustrates the developments in Britain: between 1840 and 1850, the number of people working in the transport sector doubled, and between 1850 and 1880 this figure doubled again.[30] Another consequence of this development was that it created a need for skilled workers in certain fields, such as craftsmen, engineers, plumbers and technicians of various kinds within transport and machine production. This resulted in wage inequality between the skilled and unskilled workers. The standard of living rose and social conflicts were reduced. On the other hand, living conditions and the social conditions for the unskilled were "shockingly bad" says Hobsbawn.[31]

---

[27] Hobsbawn (1968: 90).

[28] Hobsbawn (1968: 92), second footnote.

[29] For an elaboration of these three innovations in steel production, see Hobsbawn (1968: 95).

[30] Hobsbawn (1968: 95).

[31] Hobsbawn (1968: 96).

Other innovations that saw the light of day in the 1830s and 1840s were new methods of steel production, where costs and processing time fell sharply. In addition, electromagnetism and inorganic chemistry were established as the fields of science. Chemical advances were made, especially in the new university research laboratories where experiments could be carried out under optimal conditions; this played a major role in scientific technological improvements and innovation. Both electrical and chemical knowledge were produced by scientific research.[32]

A consequence of the growth in productivity in British industry in general, and steel production in particular, was a very large export of English capital to Europe, the USA and the Far East. The stock markets in Manchester, Liverpool and Glasgow were characterised as early as the 1840s by a type of mania in the speculation of shares for these new industries. A new class of rentiers entered the industrial arena, who speculated in stocks. Around 1871, i.e. just before the crash in 1873, there was said to be 170,000 people in England belonging to this new class, who had no other occupation than stock speculation and managing their rents.[33] Many of them were unmarried women or "ladies" who put their capital into private companies on the stock exchange. They often had their residences in the Swiss Alps and Tuscan cities. One can only imagine what happened to these widows and unmarried daughters of wealthy traders, when the crash came and the value of their shares was significantly reduced.

The railways and steel production made Britain the world's leading industrial nation around 1870. There was a sharp increase in the rate of innovation around the 1840s. Change came from local and private entities, rather than change or innovation through government legislation.[34] Around 1850, the expression "an English week" was established, which was a free weekend, at least from Saturday midday, and a ten-hour working day. In 1847, a new law was introduced limiting the working day to 10 hours. The practice had, however, already been established in many areas, long before the law was passed. Another innovation that boosted

---

[32] Hobsbawn (1968: 144).
[33] Hobsbawn (1968: 97).
[34] Hobsbawn (1968: 100).

productivity was a new incentive system called "piecework", i.e. workers were paid not only for the time they worked but also for the amount of work they performed during this time.

The phasing out of the mercantilist doctrine and the onset of the new spirit of the times, free trade and "laissez-faire" became the dominant economic model throughout the 1800s. Less government and more private capital was the new slogan. As competition from the rest of Europe increased, the "laissez-faire" policy came under criticism. In particular, from the growing working class, who demanded more intervention from the state, rather than just low taxes and a stable currency.[35]

Competition from the Rest of Europe

The extent of railway construction indicates how the rest of Europe challenged British industrial supremacy. Between 1850 and 1880, Britain built 11,000 miles of railway lines, whereas the rest of Europe built 76,000 miles during the same period.[36]

It is reasonable to assume that the economic progress in Britain spurred other European nations to emulate British industrialisation. The British ban on the export of machinery slowed industrialisation in the rest of Europe, but did not stop it.

Industrialisation of the rest of Europe was also hindered by the toll stations between the various markets, both in Germany, which was not unified as a nation before 1871, and in France. The customs barriers between the various production sites and markets within each country was a hindrance to industrialisation, because of increased costs that were relatively higher than in Britain, which had no such domestic tariff barriers.[37]

Another obstacle to industrialisation in continental Europe was that income inequality was much greater there than in Britain, despite the fact that Britain had a wealthy and sizeable upper class population. The upper classes in Europe were dominant from an economic perspective, and largely decided what was to be produced through their greater capacity

---

[35] Hobsbawn (1968: 199).
[36] Hobsbawn (1968: 93).
[37] Landes (2003: 125–127).

for demand, whereas the continental European middle class was not yet on a par with the British middle class. The continental European working population were poorer than their British equivalents, and mainly purchased goods that were produced locally.[38]

The capital that was accumulated in mainland Europe went largely to luxury consumption, the properties of the aristocracy and monumental buildings. In Britain, however, much of the capital accumulation was invested in emerging industry.

The USA

The extent of railway construction in the USA between 1850 and 1880, which was 99,000 miles,[39] indicates the level of industrial competition Britain was faced with from the USA up until 1873.

The crisis in the USA started with a financial panic on the stock exchange, and spread out over the entire economy. The depression was the worst thing that had happened to the American economy since the Civil War (1861–1865). The economic crisis in Europe in the 1870s and up until 1893 also greatly affected the USA. The financial panic that occurred on the stock exchange in several places in the USA in 1893 took on a greater intensity. The depression occurred while the economy was in transition from agricultural to industrial production, which was also a feature the American crisis had in common with continental Europe, whereas in Britain, it was more a case of a transition from holding a supreme position in the industrial market to competing with the rest of Europe and the USA. In other words, the crisis differed in the various countries.

Production in the USA fell to 80 % of potential capacity in the 1870s and 1890s; this applied to railway construction, machinery production and agricultural output.[40]

---

[38] Landes (2003: 129).
[39] Hobsbawn (1968: 93).
[40] Hoffmann (1970: 13; 18–19 tables).

Developments Leading to the Crisis

Dating the Great Depression to the period 1873–1897 includes Britain, the rest of Europe and the USA. In practice, however, the crisis developed differently in the various countries, and also affected different social classes in the various countries. The disagreement between economic historians concerning the length of the depression and how people and countries were affected may be explained by the fact of the different economic cycles in various countries. In the USA, the Civil War and the consequences of the war had barely subsided, when the crisis broke out. Industrialisation had not come so far as it had in Britain and several European countries. The American crisis therefore had different characteristics than in, for instance, Britain.[41]

Everything seemed to be going well for the British economy, and the British middle classes were unaware of any problems up ahead. However, the years between 1873 and 1893 (The Great Depression) in Britain were not as anticipated. The depression affected mainly the middle classes, and not to the same extent the working classes. The working classes had been hit hard by the depression in 1840, which may be termed a transformation from the first to the second phase of industrialisation[42]; they were also hit hard later by the crisis in the 1920s and 1930s.

What happened in the Great Depression, amongst other things, was that the British economy stagnated. Those who had lived lucratively on shares and interest rates had hard days in front of them; the trips to the Swiss Alps and the house in Tuscany had to be abandoned. The crisis was, however, much stronger for most people in central Europe and the USA. Share prices did not recover, and income from financial transactions was no longer so lucrative. Prices and profits fell in Britain.

The period between 1850 and 1873 was a period of strong economic growth in Europe. For instance, this concerned the considerable building of the railways, consumption of coal in industry, production of industrial goods, steamship capacity, iron and steel production and textile manu-

---

[41] Hoffmann (1970: 4).
[42] Hobsbawn (1968: 88).

facturing. Meanwhile, industry became technologically modern and more innovations that had been invented in Britain were distributed and applied.[43]

The steam engine replaced water power to a great extent. Many incremental technological innovations were made during this period. Some of these were the steam hammer, various machine applications based on steam technology, such as the steam saw. These innovations were introduced around 1840.[44] Possibly the railways were the single factor that had the greatest impact on the development of economy, culture, social relations and political conditions. With the advent of the railways, people came into contact with each other in ways that were not possible before. The railway network was first established around 1840s in Belgium; Germany around 1840–1850 and France around 1850–1860. Otherwise, the various countries of Europe had built railway lines along some of the major transport routes. Cheaper transport led to, as we have shown above, cheaper goods, as prices were forced down.

An interesting perspective is that when demand for goods increases due to new technology, this may then lead to price increases in the short term, resulting in old methods of production surviving a little longer. In other words, different production technologies could exist alongside each other until the most productive method took over. At this point, however, those enterprises that had used the old production technology would experience a much greater fall than necessary, because so many of them would go bankrupt in such a short space of time. It is at such a time that a crisis is established as a fact. This view is also supported by Landes.[45] When two production technologies operate side by side, one can imagine that there is a main driving force that drives the economy towards an ever greater focus on productivity. During the period under discussion, it is fair to say that it was the railways that literally provided the economy with a locomotive effect. The

---

[43] Landes (2003: 193).

[44] Landes (2003: 196). There was a great deal of innovations from this period that were not used until later periods. These are discussed in relation to the crisis in the 1920s.

[45] Landes (2003: 196)

old production technology with lower productivity could only survive for a short period of time, and the more it was supported by natural and political measures, the greater the fall, when the new production methods took over, driven by a locomotive effect, productivity growth and relatively declining prices.

What often inhibits the locomotive effect, which was also the case in Europe in the 1850s, is what may be designated institutions, understood as laws, rules, norms and values. These institutions often continue to operate long after they cease to have any function. They could often be counterproductive. Technological change and diffusion may be inhibited by institutional factors, such as laws and regulations, which North has shown.[46]

The free and uninhibited establishment of businesses was not necessarily something that could be taken for granted in the 1850s. The governing bureaucracy often placed major obstacles in the way of free investments concerning, for instance, new businesses that applied new technology. The first changes in this area were found in Britain around 1856–1862 and in France in 1863–1867. Germany had a more chequered past in this context, because there were many independent states prior to the unification of 1871. For instance, in Lübeck and Hamburg it had long been possible to freely establish businesses, while this did not become possible in Prussia and several other states before 1871.[47] In other words, this concerned institutional innovations that influenced the development towards the crisis in 1873. Almost simultaneously with this development, businesses in one European country were allowed to establish themselves in other European countries, which promoted competition and squeezed costs and prices down. A financial innovation that saw the light of day in the 1860s was checking accounts. Laws concerning patent rights were also introduced at this time. This made it easier to invest in a project, without risking that others imitated the idea.

---

[46] North (1993, 1994, 1997).
[47] Landes (2003: 198).

It also became easier to engage in international trade through several laws that were implemented in the 1850 and 1860s.[48] This was an expression of a change from protectionist to free trade philosophy that came to dominate economic thinking in Europe during this period. Landes says: "This cluster of trade agreements is unique in economic history."[49] The spread of free trade ideas resulted in specialisation, large-scale production and an increasing geographical division of labour, and in continental Europe being able to compete with Britain.

In continental Europe, it wasn't only free trade ideas that resulted in improved trade and thus a growing economy, transport systems were improved in various sectors, from steamships to railways. New energy sources promoted productivity. The monetary system was improved so that there was more money in circulation; more paper money, improved credit facilities and lower interest rates increased the supply of money to businesses. In addition to this, the easing of restrictions and legislation made it easier for entrepreneurs and innovators to initiate new activities.

New credit facilities, i.e. financial product innovations, meant that banks like the new factories introduced innovations into their operations. New customer groups had access to money and credit, which increased the flow of money in the market. Banks were registered as limited liability companies in Britain after 1830, and in the rest of Europe from the 1850s onwards. This increased competition for credit, which put more money into the market. Investment banks registered as limited liability companies was an innovation in continental Europe; these banks made it possible with relatively little risk to invest in innovative industrial projects.

The Crisis

The crisis in Europe began in 1873 and lasted with ups and downs until September 1896. In other words, this was an economic crisis that

---

[48] Some of the laws that promoted internal trade in Europe were those that removed restrictions on the waterways of Europe, such as the Rhine, Danube, Elbe, as well as canals, and the straits of the Baltic Sea. A single currency system within the various European countries also made trade easier. Reduction of tariffs in Europe also promoted trade (Landes 2003: 200)

[49] Landes (2003: 200).

lasted for more than 20 years. Prices declined substantially throughout the period, with a few exceptions. The general price decline in the period was approximately 33 %, which represents the biggest decline in prices known in history.[50] Deflation lasted from 1873 to 1876.[51] When prices fell, people waited before making investments and purchases, because "tomorrow" everything was expected to be cheaper. This way of thinking reinforced the crisis further. Interest rates and profits fell too. The crisis may be understood as a slow implosion, although it had different characteristics in Britain than on the continent. Prices and wages first began to rise again in 1897, and consequently optimism and consumption returned. The entrepreneur period returned, and enthusiasm spread across Europe. The collapse between 1873 and 1896 was followed by an economic breakthrough that lasted until the crisis in the 1920s. The First World War raged between the two crises; the war may also provide an explanation of why the crisis (1873–1896) has faded into history. The contrast between the crisis and the millions who died in the First World War was so great, that people tend to remember the war, but forget the crisis, which after all was not so terrible.

In the USA, the crisis began with the stock market crash (called the "Panic of 1893"); it was followed by a rebound later in 1893. Banks went bankrupt, and many shareholders lost everything they owned (507 different banks went bankrupt in 1893).[52] In addition, several other lending institutions collapsed. From summer 1893 to summer 1894, the crisis spread to manufacturing companies throughout the country. Then a panic was set off in June 1894, which was followed by an upturn in 1895. After this, there was a sharp decline that lasted until June 1897.[53] The crisis in the USA followed a double curve, like two camel humps. This was a depression which was great and lasted for 5

[50] Landes (2003: 231).
[51] Landes (2003: 233).
[52] Hoffmann (1970: 67).
[53] Hoffmann (1970: 47–48).

years. Millions of families were greatly affected by the economic down-turn in the USA[54]; Unemployment and strikes were rampant.

Analysis

Institutional Innovations

The repeal regarding the law forbidding the export of industrial machinery for the textile industry, and the free establishment of businesses (1850s–1860s) characterises the dominant liberal atti-tudes in Europe towards economic and social processes. The above repeal meant that British industry could profit by their expertise in developing machinery, and in the long term this led to competition between Britain and the rest of Europe; this increased productivity and along with other factors mentioned above helped to force prices down (which also contributed to deflation during the crisis in Europe [1873–1896]).

The free establishment of businesses resulted in some thriving, while others went bankrupt with consequences for employment and social con-ditions. The patent law was extended to include "trade marks" (1860s), which increased the desire for investment and thus the dynamics of trade and industry, i.e. "dynamics" may be understood by the fact that more businesses were able to come into the market, though some would go bankrupt.

Industrialisation on the European continent led to the growth of a new industrial working class that played a dominant role in the 1800s in the development of society.

The unification of Germany (1871) resulted in tariff barriers being reduced and partly disappearing in large parts of what had before con-stituted the North and South German Confederations, increasing trade and competition.

---

[54] Hoffmann (1970: 67).

Economic Innovations

There were many financial innovations in the period leading up to the economic crisis, the railways being perhaps the single most important regarding development during this period; major capital inflow and speculation led to capital profit opportunities in railway construction and the infrastructure around the railways. At the same time, steam gradually replaced sail in shipping. The economic activities in the transport sector that competed with railways and steamships were steam rolled by these two innovations over a period of time. Bankruptcies, reallocations of resources, expertise and people moving from one area to other areas affected and drove the economy towards a transformation; it is reasonable to assume that it was the railways and steamships that literally provided the locomotive effect of this transformation process. In addition to these two economic locomotive effects, there were several other smaller locomotive effects that drove the economy into a transformational crisis. For instance, the telegraph, new ways of producing steel[55] and the chemical industries were driving forces in this process. In addition to these, there were a number of financial innovations that contributed to the transformation, for instance, new credit facilities, amongst others, for checking accounts that made it easier for people to buy goods and services. Investment banks were registered as limited liability companies that also made it possible to allocate capital more easily, which could be applied to investments in new innovations and other profit opportunities.

Reflection

In the period 1890–1895, the USA and Germany produced more steel than Britain, which suggests that the Long Depression had serious consequences for Britain. Britain had been the "workshop of the world" prior to the Long Depression, while after the Long Depression there

---

[55] The Bessemer Converter.

were metaphorically speaking many "workshops" in the world. Britain no longer led the world industrialisation and economic growth; the crisis had resulted in Central Europe, with Germany in the lead and the USA becoming central economic actors threatening Britain's position.

The crisis of 1873–1896 is more difficult and more complex than, say, the Tulip Bubble, the South Sea Bubble or the Mississippi Bubble. One of the reasons for this is the different course of development the crisis had in the various countries which it struck. Another reason is the many institutional and financial innovations that led to the crisis. Regardless of this complexity, one can say with a high degree of probability that there were three main driving forces behind the crisis of 1873–1896. Concerning the institutional innovations, it is reasonable to assume that it was the liberal ideas in many areas of society that led to the crisis. As far as the economic innovations were concerned, it is reasonable to say that it was the railways and steam engine that drove the economy towards a transformation, where the old production and transportation methods were replaced with new ones. When the new breakthrough emerged and began to play an increasingly large role in economic life, a transformation occurred that resulted in those who were connected to the old and established methods of production, distribution and consumption being pushed aside. In other words, there was a more or less simultaneous process of breakthroughs and breakdowns, an economic crisis, in this case the Long/Great Depression. One might be tempted to take a figure from European literature, and say that what seems like economic paradise, namely innovations which result in "everyone" becoming richer, is actually like Dante's Inferno: you have to go through the inferno and cleanse your soul before going to heaven. This is not unlike the idea that it is in the collapse that one catches a glimpse of the breakthrough.

The above analysis and description is illustrated in Fig. 5.1.

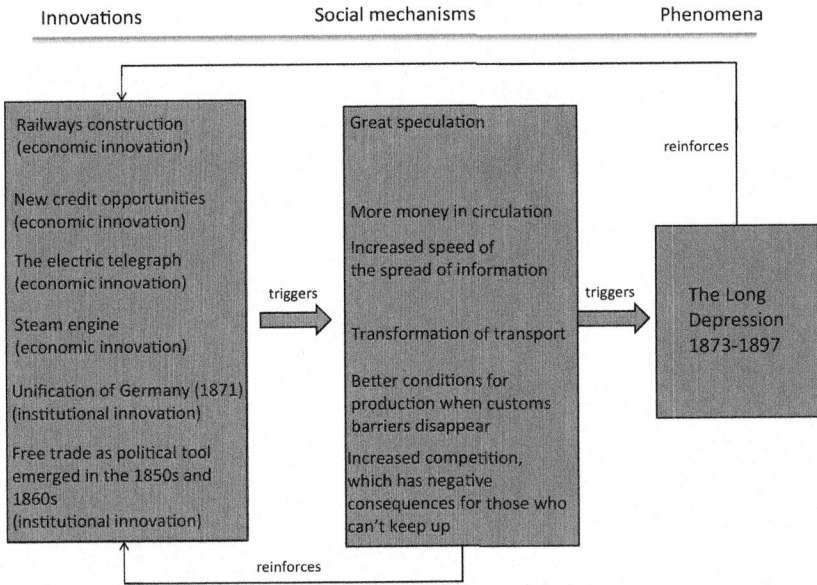

Fig. 5.1   The Long Depression

6

The Great Depression of the 1930s

Introduction

The crisis of 1929 may be said to resemble the Tulip, South Sea and the Mississippi Bubbles, more than it does with the Long Depression of 1873–1896. First is the similarity concerning the fact that these crises were all triggered on specific dates; second, it is possible to see how they spread; and third, the consequences are relatively easy to identify.

Most people who know a little history can associate specific historical events with dates such as 1776, 1914 and 1939. Similarly, the year 1929 is burned into our historical consciousness. Some may even know which month in 1929 is worth remembering, October; and those who are more than a little interested may know what day in October it was, namely a Thursday, which goes by the name of Black Thursday. Some people may also know the specific date as if it concerned the outbreak of a war—24 October 1929—which was the day when share prices on the New York Stock Exchange collapsed, with great consequences, economically, socially, politically and, from a longer perspective, armed global conflict. This involved an economic crisis which lasted roughly 10 years and ended with the start of World War II.

© The Author(s) 2017   **111**
J.-A. Johannessen, *Innovations Lead to Economic Crises*,
DOI 10.1007/978-3-319-41793-6_6

People who bought shares in 1929 and hadn't sold them before the onset of the crisis, lost what they had invested. The crisis affected all Western industrialized countries. Instability and large sales marked the days before stock prices crashed. Central bankers stepped in to stabilize share prices by buying large blocks of shares at a higher price than the market demanded. This strategy had been shown to be effective in taking control of a nascent stock fall in 1907. However, in 1929, this strategy only stabilized the market temporarily. On Black Thursday, 24 October, many people would not invest in stocks anymore and sold out, and stock prices fell by 13%. On 29 October, there were several large investors who offered support by buying shares to stabilize the market. On 30 October, the stock market went up by 12%. However, this didn't help. The market continued to fall in the days to come. Panic spread. Rumours began to swirl around. Everyone wanted to get out of the stock market. The crisis on the New York Stock Exchange was now a fact. On 13 November, the stock exchange reached a temporary plateau. The market rose from then up until April 17, 1930. It then began to fall again and eventually bottomed out on 8 July 1932 with a final fall from its peak in September 1929 of 89% of its value. After this, the share value rose for most of the 1930s, but did not reach the value attained on 3 September 1929, until 23 November 1954.

Background and Developments Prior to Crisis

The 10-year period leading up to the Wall Street Crash of 1929 was one of economic growth in the Western industrialized world; over a 9-year period up until October 1929, the Dow Jones index increased tenfold, albeit with minor setbacks. These falls in the stock market, such as in 1920–1921,[1] led to panic, but only lasted a short time, after which growth continued. Underlying real production conditions were also improved.

---

[1] Galbraith (2009: 31). The panic or crisis was the result of agricultural prices falling sharply, although costs remained high.

All wars are inflationary, says Landes.[2] World War I was no exception. After the war, the controls and restrictions that had been imposed during the war were removed, the dam burst and prices began to rise sharply. Prices reached a peak in Britain in 1920, where the average price level was about two to two and a half times as high as it had been during the pre-war period. In France, much of its production capabilities had been destroyed by the war; consequently prices continued to rise until 1926–1927, by roughly 300% compared to pre-war levels. However, the worst cases of inflation occurred in Germany, Austria and Eastern Europe. In Austria, for example, prices rose by 1400% (as measured by the level of 1913 = 100), and in Hungary and Poland, matters were even worse. However, the worst effects of inflation were witnessed in Germany, especially, which was forced to pay war reparations, amongst other things, towards the re-construction of France after World War I; consequently, prices rose by an unfathomable amount. Landes writes that by 1923, "the mark was worth one trillionth of its pre-war value."[3] The printing presses for banknotes in Germany could hardly print money fast enough to keep up with the rising inflation. There were many inventions and innovations from the mid-1800s onwards that did not become significant until later; many of these affected the crisis of 1920 and beyond into the 1930s. One of these was the Bessemer Converter (1856), which made steel production cheaper and more efficient.[4] Other financial innovations that came into general use in the early 1900s were the industrial use of electricity, the gas engine, etc.[5] These innovations laid the foundation for economic growth throughout the 1920s, but carried within them the seeds of the economic crisis in the sense that they led to major economic transformations in established production and distribution methods.

From 1920 until 1929, there was a very high level of investment in steel production. Steel was necessary for the building of bridges and skyscrapers, etc. Automotive production also rose sharply during this

---

[2] Landes (2003: 361).

[3] Landes (2003: 362).

[4] Tracy (2005).

[5] For an overview of the technological innovations that became common at the beginning of the twentieth century, see Fig. 1.

period.[6] Production was also organised in a new way, under the "Scientific Management" method; Taylorism was also influential in the 1920s. These were organizational innovations that linked up with the new economic innovations. We should also remember that part of the world market was closed off from the capitalist world after the establishment of the Soviet Union in 1917. This may be understood as an institutional, political innovation, with some trade being re-channelled into other markets. Although this institutional innovation affected the market, it must not be over emphasized, because Russia was primarily an agricultural country at the time, and only integrated into Western industrialisation processes to a small degree.

Perhaps the main innovation involved specialisation in machine production; machines were also used to produce other machines. The aforementioned organisational innovations streamlined production, making mass production more efficient, and led to increased productivity, cheaper products, higher profits and wages, and expectations of a better future for all.[7]

Optimism characterized the 1920s; "the rich were getting richer much faster than the poor were getting less poor," writes Galbraith.[8] Although many were still poor in the industrialized world, this was a period when there were expectations of increased prosperity. Many also climbed up the social ladder to the middle class and made a good life for themselves in material terms. Production increased and millions of Americans and Europeans were able to buy a car for the first time.[9] Higher incomes and better transport also led to a change in the zeitgeist. Galbraith writes that many people wanted to get rich quick without working hard for their money,[10] driving many people into stock speculation; consequently, it may be argued that a speculation-driven economy became part of the zeitgeist. Real estate investments in Florida are perhaps indicative of this spirit of the times; speculation and a sharp increase in real estate prices

---

[6] In 1926 as many as 4,301,000 were produced. In 1929, production had risen to 5,358,000 (Wilson 1948: 141).

[7] Hobsbawn (1968: 146).

[8] Galbraith (2009: 31).

[9] Wilson (1948).

[10] Galbraith (2009: 32).

in what was called "America's Riviera" led to a belief amongst middle class people that they could become rich not so much by hard work, but by speculating in real estate. Interestingly, when the Florida Bubble burst in 1925, this did not diminish the belief in the stock market, rather the opposite. However, the 1920s was by no means a decade without problems; amongst other things, as mentioned, when the Florida Bubble popped this was a signal that something was about to happen. In 1926 "The Times" production index fell sharply,[11] but quickly recovered. Confidence in the market's ability to adjust itself was strengthened. Continued speculation and over-investment when the possibility of quick money could be envisioned would seem to suggest that speculation was out of control; however, Galbraith writes that after 1927 this wasn't the case.[12] In the context of this chapter, as mentioned, it is important to note that speculation and access to making fast money became an accepted part of the zeitgeist, which might be described as a rewriting of Weber's Protestant work ethic. It is reasonable to assume that such thinking as described above was also part of the causal complex of the South Sea, Mississippi and Tulip Bubbles.

From 1927, stock market prices rose almost continuously. This was also the year when the innovative Ford Model T was superseded by the Model A, which had been developed by incremental innovations. However, the end of the Model T production was first perceived by the market as signalling a downturn in the market; yet when the Model A was launched the "Times" production index swung up sharply.[13]

Expectations of earnings on invested money seemed to heighten speculation on the stock exchange; it was the expectation of earning on investments without seemingly great risk that drove up the stock market; when these expectations were met, they reinforced a further rise. When the stock market started to fall in 1928, there seemed to be expectations that the market would rise again, shrug off the unrest and continue to rise. Very few people saw the crisis approaching, 1 year before the stock market collapsed. It may seem as if the zeitgeist encouraged people to ignore

---

[11] The index fell from 181 in early 1926 to 143 in March 1926 (Galbraith 2009: 36).
[12] Galbraith (2009: 39).
[13] The index at the end of 1927 was 245 (Galbraith 2009: 37).

the reality that began to make itself visible. It was apparent to most people that something was happening because the newspapers wrote about a "boiling" market.[14] Of course, it is when the market is boiling that there are also opportunities to make large profits on the stock exchanges. In other words, the ethos of the age seemed to drive speculation further, and the market continued to boil. No one was interested in turning down the heat to lower the temperature, figuratively speaking.

If it is true that the basic way of thinking at the time was the expectation of earning a lot of money quickly, then this can lead to a feeling of omnipotence in an overheated market. It was something like this that happened in 1928. Everyone wanted to make a profit on the stock market. As a result, the market began to boil over. On the other hand, it is possible to argue that this was an expression of the positive aspects of the market. The point is that this development led to over-investment in some areas, so the market seemed to "spin around itself".

If one measures the degree of "speculation" as the proportion of borrowed money behind each invested dollar, pound, etc., then it was very large, and it grew from 1926 to the end of 1928. The return on invested capital was roughly 12% on the stock exchanges in the United States. This meant that capital flowed to the stock market. The banks were able to borrow from the Federal Reserve at 4%, and then lend this money to market speculators at 12%.[15] "Everyone" envisioned the opportunity of becoming rich without making much of an effort. The ethos of the age also had an effect on the "work mentality". The conflict between those who had trouble finding work and those who had expectations of wealth are expressed by Galbraith: "Never had there been a better time to get rich".[16]

In 1925 Britain went back to the gold standard at the pre-World War 1 relationship between gold, the dollar and the pound. The result was that British goods were bought with a high-valued pound, at prices that reflected wartime inflation. Other countries were obviously reluctant to purchase such highly priced British goods, though it was easy to sell goods

---

[14] Galbraith (2009: 40).
[15] Galbraith (2009: 48).
[16] Galbraith (2009: 50).

to Britain at this exchange rate.[17] A general strike was held in Britain in 1926 due to circumstances related to this problem.

Historians and economists debate today whether the Wall Street Crash of 1929 was the cause of the economic crisis, or a symptom of the underlying factors.[18] However, we know for a fact that the first three decades of the 1900s were characterised by the application of innovations that led to electrification, automation of factories, mass production of industrial goods and the motorization of agriculture; these innovations increased productivity dramatically, reduced the cost per unit of goods and also resulted in higher wages and fewer working hours per week around 1919 in several countries.

In the late 1800s and early 1900s, there was a stream of inventions and innovations that were discovered, implemented, spread and accepted by the market.[19] These were institutional and economic innovations related to production, processing, transport and consumption, and they included the steam turbine, the light bulb, the discovery of electromagnetic waves, the radio, the telephone, ammonia synthesis, aspirin, assembly lines, electric motors (such as those in vehicles), electrification of trains, diesel engines after 1890, the first aircraft, tractors, etc. The time lag between an invention and its use as an innovation in a market is relatively long, sometimes as much as 40 years,[20] which provides one explanation of the time lag between the introduction of inventions and the eruption of an economic crisis.

The Crisis and Explanations

The Crisis

The crash began on October 29, 1929. Some economic historians and economists argue that it was the rigidity of the gold standard that resulted

---

[17] Galbraith (2009: 38).
[18] Frank and Bernanke (2007: 98).
[19] Smil (2005: 10)
[20] Van Dujin (1983).

in the crisis spreading so rapidly; indeed, in 1931, Britain, Japan and the Scandinavian countries all left the gold standard. Many argue that it was precisely the abolition of the gold standard that made it possible to recover relatively quickly;[21] by 1936 all the major countries had abandoned the gold standard.

Foreign trade fell by roughly 50% and unemployment was between 25% and 33% in many countries.[22] Urban areas were hit the hardest, because this was where the heavy industry was located, such as the steel industry. Agriculture also suffered, and prices fell by roughly 60%.[23] Retail prices in the major Western countries fell by 23% to 46%.[24] Just after the crisis, in 1930, consumer demand decreased by roughly 10%, while public sector demand increased. It may be argued that the government tried to keep the wheels of the economy running, while the private sector wanted to save its way through the crisis.[25] In the mid-1930s, interest rates were sharply reduced, private demand decreased, and expectations of deflation hindered investment. This resulted, among other things, in industrial production falling in various countries between 23% and 46%.[26] Deflation began to be felt around 1931.[27] The decline in the American economy was the anchor that dragged down the economies of other countries. Some writers believe that protectionist measures in the United States and other countries reinforced the economic downturn, because trade slowed very sharply.[28]

---

[21] Eichengren (1992).

[22] Frank and Bernanke (2007: 98).

[23] Cochrane (1958: 15).

[24] In the United States the retail prices from 1929 to 1932 fell by 32 %, while the figures for Britain were 33 %, France 34 % and Germany 29 % (Jerome et al. 1970: 885).

[25] Frank and Bernanke (2007: 98).

[26] In the United States, industrial production between 1929 and 1932 fell by 46%, while the figures for England were 23 %, France 24 % and Germany 41 % (Jerome et al. 1970: 885).

[27] Hamilton (1987: 145–169).

[28] In the United States, foreign trade fell by 70 % between 1929 and 1932, while the figures for England were 60 %, France 54 % and Germany 61 % (Jerome et al. 1970: 885).

Explanations

There are two main categories of theories that attempt to explain the crisis of the 1930s, and each has its subgroups. The first category may be termed demand-driven theories; this includes Keynesian explanations,[29] but also theories related to trade. The institutional economists[30] argue that the crisis was a result of under-consumption and over-investment, which led to an economic bubble.

The second category of explanations refers to the monetary aspects of the crisis; the monetarists often point to structural problems related to monetary policy. For instance, they point out that the Federal Reserve tightened the flow of money into the market, when it should have adopted expansionary measures.[31]

Those who argue that business cycles of various types are a normal part of economic development, say that wave theories provide the basis for an explanation of the crisis. From this perspective, the stock market crash was just a symptom of the underlying waves.[32]

The Keynesian explanation of the crisis is that the overall level of activity was too low, i.e. the total level of activity measured as a function of private consumption, investment, government consumption and net exports. The Keynesian position is that when the economy was in the throws of the crisis, the government should have increased its consumption to maintain the total level of consumption and employment.[33]

As the crisis continued, the American president, Franklin Delano Roosevelt, increased public spending through the "New Deal" programme, which involved public infrastructure projects and subsidies to farmers[34] amongst other measures.

---

[29] Markwell (2006).
[30] Coase (1992: 713–719).
[31] Butler (2011).
[32] Dal Pont (2013).
[33] Klein (1947: 56–58); 177–178.
[34] Rosenof (1997).

Several writers have claimed that the "Smoot-Hawley Tariff Act" of 17 June 1930[35] exacerbated the crisis, because it reduced trade; this protectionist policy also spread to other countries, which further worsened the crisis. When American farmers faced tariff barriers in the countries they exported to, this led to a reduction of roughly 50% in American agricultural exports, contributing to bankruptcies in agriculture and the banking sector.

Irving Fisher[36] developed a theory explaining that the crisis in 1929 was generated by loans,[37] arguing that investments were financed by loans, which drove up speculation and led to a bubble in the economy. When the crisis was established, banks and moneylenders demanded repayment of these loans, but those who had borrowed money were unable to pay; this resulted in bankruptcy for the borrowers and collapse for the banks. When deflation set in, it was even more difficult for people to repay their loans, which worsened the economic downturn. Ten months after the crash of 1929, 744 banks had declared bankruptcy in the United States.[38] The panic had led to the banks demanding the payment of outstanding loans, which people were not able to repay, and the downturn became ever more deeply entrenched in the economic system.

The Austrian School[39] argue that the economic crisis was the outcome of the policies of the Federal Reserve (est. 1913); in their view, the crisis was a credit-driven economic bubble that developed in the 1920s,[40] and was made possible through the flow of money to private consumption and investment. By the time the Federal Reserve limited the cash inflow (in 1928) it was too late:[41] the "loan-locomotive" had been set in motion, and it could not be stopped before it crashed in October 1929. The Austrian economists believe that government intervention to deal

---

[35] This Act raised customs fees on more than 20,000 imported goods. The result was the import of goods into the United States fell by roughly 50 % (Merill 1990: 340).

[36] Fisher originated the theory in 1933, but it was published in a separate book in 2011 (see Fisher 1933; 2011)

[37] For every dollar invested, nine dollars were borrowed.

[38] Friedman and Schwartz (1971: 352)

[39] Hagemann et al. (2010).

[40] Rothbard (2011: 19–21).

[41] Rothbard (2011: 159–163).

with the crisis only prolonged it, because the market was not allowed to regulate itself.[42]

Marxist economists hold the view that under free market capitalism there will always be times when the accumulation rate of capital is high, because profits will be high in some areas of the economy. The imbalance in the rate of capital accumulation leads to over-investment in some capital goods, and under-consumption of other capital goods. The Marxists reason that this follows from the unequal distribution of the means of wealth creation in society, leading to periodic crises. Periodic crises, or "business cycles", are also emphasized by Schumpeter, who borrowed his term "creative destruction" from Karl Marx.[43] While Marxists focus on capital accumulation, Schumpeterians focus on innovations as drivers of productivity and economic growth. Creative destruction is understood in this context as the process through which the new and creative emerges from a source of destruction such as a financial crisis or a war.

In 1937, 8 years after the crisis, about 20% of the American workforce was still unemployed.[44] Keynes' view that an economy could be in balance but still have high unemployment[45] seemed to be the case in the United States at this time.

Analysis

Institutional Innovations

An important institutional innovation in the period leading up to 1929 was the Russian Revolution of 1917, which resulted in, amongst others things, the establishment of the Soviet Union. It also resulted in a shrinking of the so-called capitalist market. However, it is possible that this institutional innovation played only a minor role in the evolution towards the crisis in 1929: the Soviet Union at that time was a backward

[42] Rothbard (2011: 19–21).
[43] Marx and Engels (2002: 226); Marx 1993/1857: 750; Marx 1969/1863: 495–496).
[44] Forster and Magdoff (2009: 13).
[45] Keynes cited in Galbraith (1977: 216).

rural area, where industrial innovations had not been introduced to any great extent. Nevertheless, the future market for industrial goods was restricted by the Russian Revolution.

The institutional, cultural innovation that developed at the same time as the economic innovations (which it is reasonable to assume had great significance for the crisis in 1929) was what may be here described as the ethos of the age, namely the idea that people believed they could get rich quickly without hard work; one consequence was that people speculated in the new innovations that emerged. This further promoted the desire to speculate and encouraged capital allocation and accumulation in those areas speculators believed would be profitable.

Economic Innovations

There were many economic innovations, and they transformed the entire economic sector between 1867 and 1929. When innovations were adopted they underwent continuous improvements. In this way, confidence in the market for these innovations grew continuously. The innovations we are talking about here are essentially what is known as economic innovations, which are technological, service, organizational and marketing innovations. The most important innovations here were light bulbs, the telephone, aluminium production, typewriters, electricity, photography, motorcycles, cars, steel constructions, assembly lines, film, tractors, aircraft, the radio, etc. A new civilisation was building up on the basis of these innovations, as Smil writes.[46]

When it comes to inventions and innovations, it appears that a threshold must be exceeded before an innovation penetrates the market. When these thresholds are exceeded, clusters of innovations emerge, and they eventually become part of people's everyday lives.

In 1800, the wooden plough was the most common tool used for ploughing fields, although iron ploughs had been invented a considerable time before this date. Similarly, even though steamships were first in practical use at the beginning of the 1800s, sailing ships remained the

---

[46] Smil (2005: 259–303).

most common form of commercial shipping until later in the century. But suddenly, like a dam breaking, an innovation is accepted by the market, and the new breakthrough is made. Thus the iron plough eventually replaced the wooden one, and steam replaced sail.

It appears that the desire to invest follows the innovations. Capital is drawn away from established businesses, and into the new ones about to break through the barrier to entry. When a motorised tractor that can replace over a dozen horses, and the Haber-Bosch method for producing fertilizers for agriculture were taken into use, this led to a strong increase in agricultural productivity,[47] which in turn resulted in a surplus agricultural workforce which could be used in industry. Innovations led not only to increased productivity, but also to considerable urban growth. Farm workers became industrial workers, and a new class of workers organized themselves in new ways.

Reflection

The Post-World War I (1918–1929) society and economy was transformed into something completely different in relation to the 1800s; the innovations adopted by the market made production, distribution and consumption more efficient, productive and profitable. The production system was more reliable, as it had been proven and tested in practice. The following economic areas were completely transformed during this period: the energy sector, the electricity sector, new materials saw the light of day, industrial organisation increased productivity sharply, the transport sector for goods and passengers was transformed, and communication and information flow were greatly improved,[48]

The above description and analysis is shown in Fig. 6.1.

---

[47] Smil (2005: 27).
[48] Smil (2006).

Innovations   Social mechanisms   Phenomena

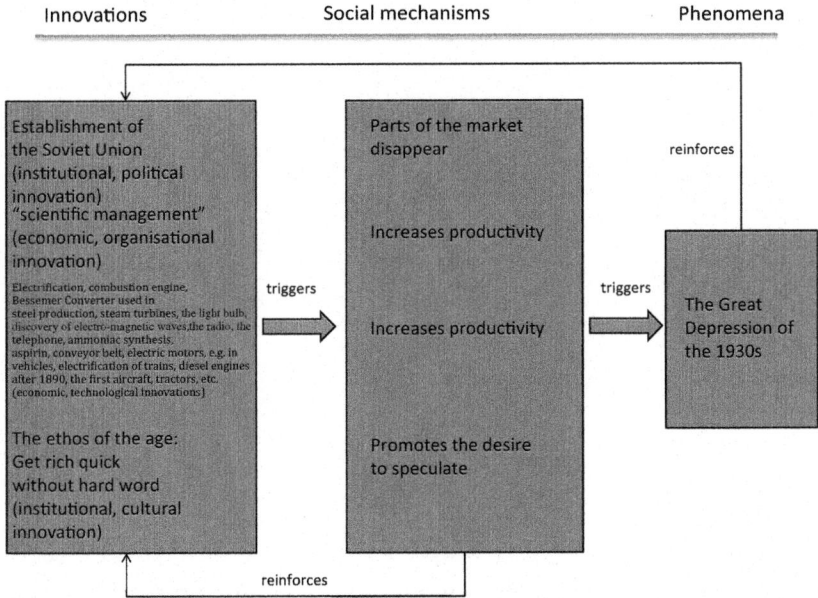

Fig. 6.1 The Great Depression of the 1930s

7

The Long Recession 2008–?

Introduction

Paul Krugman, the Nobel Prize winner in Economic Sciences, has more than suggested[1] that since in 2008 we have been in a crisis that may be compared with the major economic crises in history. The current crisis started to develop in August 2007 with the American subprime mortgage crisis, and continued to develop in 2008. In September 2008, depositors lined up outside Northern Rock Bank in the UK to withdraw all of their savings[2]; they believed the bank was going bankrupt, and they didn't want to lose their money. Fear spread quickly affecting the trust *between* banks, and the credit market between banks started to stumble. Also in September 2008, Lehman Brothers Holdings Inc. declared bankruptcy.[3] The crisis spread within two months from "Wall Street" to "Main Street" (as the everyday economy is called in the USA). What is known as

---

[1] Krugman in the *New York Times*, 26 October 2008, under the headline: "Desperately seeking seriousness".

[2] In April 2013 there was queuing outside the Cypriot banks for the same reason.

[3] Archibugi and Filippetti (2012: 9).

© The Author(s) 2017
J.-A. Johannessen, *Innovations Lead to Economic Crises*,
DOI 10.1007/978-3-319-41793-6_7

the "Minsky moment[4]", when a financial system changes from a robust system into a weak system—and is just waiting to collapse—is what was about to happen at the end of 2008.

It is reasonable to assume that explanations are guided by which perspective one takes. Thus if a financial perspective is adopted, then financial instruments may provide the main part of an explanation for the 2008 crisis. A real estate perspective would most likely focus on the subprime loans and house price bubble in the USA, which seems reasonable, because it was the US housing bubble that triggered the crisis. A banking perspective may argue that it was banks' over-eagerness to lend money, and customers' willingness to borrow, which caused the crisis. A political perspective may highlight the disagreements between different perceptions and ways of thinking. The chapter will adopt an innovation perspective.

People are beginning to agree that the current crisis started with a financial crisis around 2007.[5] The financial crisis that lasted from 2007 to roughly 2009 developed, however, into a major economic crisis, when private demand slowed. Another result was the ballooning of unemployment and deficits in public finances in several countries, including those in Southern Europe. Consequently, after 2009, it was no longer possible to speak of a unilateral financial crisis, but rather a classical production and unemployment crisis.

We were given an indication that something was brewing when the stock market fell by 95 % in Thailand in 1997,[6] and in 2000 when the Dot.com Bubble indicators of things to come. In the latter, one of the greatest technological innovations ("personal computers and internet") led to people buying shares in what they believed had underlying real value in the hope of becoming rich quickly. When the Dot.com Bubble burst the Federal Reserve reacted by cutting interest rates from 6.5 % to 3.5 % over the course of a few months.[7] After 11 September 2001, the "War on Terror" was launched; by 2003, the interest rate had been

---

[4] Minsky (1975, 1986).
[5] Macdonald (2012: 1–3).
[6] Duncan (2012: 6).
[7] Soros (2009: xv) (introduction).

reduced to 1 %. Inexpensive loans laid the foundation for the housing bubble that would burst in 2008. Everyone borrowed from the banks because it was so inexpensive. The requirements for obtaining loans were also made less stringent, and more and more people entered the housing market.

Investment banks developed new innovations which further increased credit in the global market. Pension funds and other large money management funds bought new financial instruments in the hope of earning more than could be gained in interest-rate-based products. From 2000 to 2005, writes Soros, the market values of houses and properties grew by more than 50 % in the USA, while wages rose only marginally. Half of the American GDP growth came from the appreciation of the housing and fixtures.[8] This strengthens the assumption that financial operations, for example, higher credit growth, affect underlying market prices.

People without substantial income received loans, so-called subprime loans. It is reasonable to assume that the thinking of the lenders was that if these people could get a lower entrance fee to the housing market, they could eventually sell the property, after perhaps two years, with a handsome profit and buy something else. Thus, the thinking at the time was that everyone would benefit from the subprime loans; the premise of this thinking, however, was of course that house prices would continue to rise.

In addition to the subprime loans banks developed financial product innovations, which consisted of the banks packaging the subprime loans into innovative financial instruments.[9] These financial innovations were then sold in the global market, the purpose of the geographic spread being to reduce risk. As we know today, the risk was not diminished but rather increased, because it triggered serially connected explosions that had global implications. Many investors had no idea what they bought. One must assume that most sellers did not know what risks their products had. The sellers, however, knew, that the more such products they sold, the higher bonuses they received. In 2005, it became something of a mania to try to secure oneself by using the new financial instruments

[8] Soros (2009: xv) (introduction)
[9] These instruments were termed "collateralized debt obligations" (CDOs).

called collateralised debt obligations (CDOs); this resulted in roughly 50 % of all trading in financial instruments in 2005 being related to attempts to secure oneself in one way or another.[10] Signs that something was horribly wrong began to emerge in 2007.

In August 2007, the Federal Reserve intervened on behalf of the banks to provide liquidity, so that they would avoid bankruptcy. The same thing happened in Europe. Banks were furnished with liquidity to save them from bankruptcy. A little more than a year later, on 13 September 2008, Northern Rock, one of the largest property banks in England, declared that it was not solvent. On 15 September 2008, Lehman Brothers Holdings Inc. went bankrupt. The crisis was now an established fact. As a result of the crisis that was triggered in 2007 and accelerated in 2008, 14 million Americans had become unemployed, while 9 million could only find part-time jobs in 2012.[11] In 2013, Spain had a roughly 60 % unemployment rate in 2013 among those aged 18–25 years; the situation is similar in Greece. In addition to unemployment, people are remaining out of work for longer periods than in previous recessions, and millions of Americans have lost their homes as a result of the crisis. House prices have also dropped by more than 30 % in the USA. In reality, there occurred a nationalisation of the debt in the real estate market, by placing Fannie Mae and Freddie Mac into conservatorship.[12]

The current crisis is not linked to the banking or financial system as such. One could argue, as Alan Blinder[13] does, that the crisis was triggered by the subprime loans crisis in the USA in 2007. At the time of writing in June 2013, however, the crisis is not specific for one single sector. It has reached the auto industry in the USA, the construction industry in Spain, large parts of the Greek economy, the banking sector in Cyprus in March 2013 and so on. In other words, it is not possible to call the current crisis a financial crisis, because it is not so much the financial world that is experiencing a crisis anymore, but rather production and employment. When 60 % of young people in Spain are

---

[10] Soros (2009: xviii) (introduction)
[11] Duncan (2012a: 85).
[12] Duncan (2012a: 86).
[13] Blinder (2013).

unemployed, then it would be more appropriate to call it an "employment" crisis, thereby highlighting its similarity to other major depressions throughout history.

The crisis spread from the USA, which was the epicentre, to Europe. Icelandic banks collapsed, with consequences for depositors in, amongst other countries, the Netherlands and Britain. Hungary's largest bank was on the brink of bankruptcy. Banks and financial institutions in Asia, Eastern Europe and Australia also felt the effects of the global financial earthquake with its epicentre in the USA. Turkey, South Africa and China were also affected by the consequences of the crisis.[14] One of the explanations for the rate of spread is the globalisation of financial capital that has occurred since 1973. The close connections and rapidity of information flows allowed the melt down to occur almost instantaneously throughout the world. The crisis can no longer be defined nationally or regionally. The new innovations of globalisation, new financial instruments, personal computers and the internet, enabled the crisis to be disseminated rapidly and the consequences to be felt more deeply, because many are affected at the same time.

The current crisis is often compared with the crisis in the 1930s. However, the historian Nelson writes that it is more appropriate to compare the current crisis with the Long Depression of 1873–1897.[15] An important point in this context is that if one adopts the wrong model, then any corrective measures that are implemented will be inappropriate.

It can be argued that the financial crisis of 2007 led to a demand crisis which in turn led to a production crisis, an unemployment crisis, and a possible social and political crisis. We have already seen social crises in Greece and Spain, but at the time of writing we have not yet seen any severe political crisis.

Within a crisis, to use a term from Schumpeter, there is creative destruction, which destroys the old, giving way to the new and creative, which Florida also uses in describing the ongoing crisis.[16]

---

[14] Soros (2009: 161–164).

[15] Nelson (2008: B98).

[16] Florida (2010: 4, 12).

Perhaps there is a new bubble developing, a dollar bubble? Like all bubbles, a dollar bubble would have consequences, as Duncan[17] points out. He makes a very interesting observation when he indicates that share prices rose after the quantitative measures, quantitative easing number one (QE1)—QE3, which were implemented by the American Federal Reserve, and were followed by a subsequent increase in food prices.

Soros,[18] Duncan[19] and several others[20] agree on the social mechanism that drives this crisis: credit growth and people's willingness to borrow money. Soros' hypothesis is that several bubbles were/are involved in the crisis we are now in. It is not just a housing bubble that burst in the USA, but also other bubbles that are growing.[21] The housing bubble is just a detonator which caused the serially connected bubbles to burst, figuratively speaking. When the serially connected bubbles burst, more or less simultaneously, it is reasonable to assume that this would result in the development of a depression in the global economy.

Past crises have shown that breakdown and breakthrough follow each other as economic dimensions. An economic crisis does not only have negative features, but also fosters the possibility of transforming the economic system and society into something new.

What is new in the global economy is that the rate of diffusion is so rapid. A high degree of debt coupled to a high level of commercial activity appears to be correlated with banking crises.[22] How can one increase the desire to invest for gain after the bubble has burst? In 2008, the satirical magazine "The Onion" wrote in a headline: "Recession—Plagued Nation Demands New Bubble to Invest In".[23] Bubbles may appear to be a way of maintaining the desire to invest. Chorafas asks a controversial question regarding the current crisis: "Are we running out of bubbles?"[24]

---

[17] Duncan (2012).
[18] Soros (2009: x) (Introduction)
[19] Duncan (2012, 2012a).
[20] Brunnermeier (2009); Crotty (2009); Roubini and Mihm (2010); amongst many others.
[21] Soros (2009: xi) (Introduction)
[22] Reinert and Rogoff (2010).
[23] Referred to in Foster and Magdoff (2009: 7).
[24] Chorafas (2009: 3).

First, the Dot.com Bubble burst around 2000, and then the Subprime Bubble burst in 2007–2008. It is perhaps understandable that satirists in "The Onion" and Chorafas ask for more bubbles to invest in. The underlying idea is perhaps that the economy cannot survive on sound investments alone. On top of all this, various authorities are communicating that this time cannot be compared with all the previous times. "This time it's different", they say, in the financial system, in political circles and in academia. "This time we have control" is the rhetoric they use.[25]

One can agree with Schumpeter when he says that "History is a record of 'effects' the vast majority of which nobody intended to produce".[26] The crisis we are now experiencing is of this type: no one had any intention of producing such a situation. The crisis that manifested itself in 2007–2008 was not a unique phenomenon. We have experienced the debt crisis in the 1980s. The New York Stock Exchange almost collapsed in 1987. In the 1990s, we witnessed the long Japanese stagnation and financial crises in Asia in 1997–1998. We have also mentioned the Dot.com crisis in 2000. All these events were crises that had economic and social consequences.

The chapter is organised as follows. First, I will review the current knowledge concerning the relationships between innovations and economic crises. Second, I will then describe and discuss the background and the evolution towards the crisis, and the crisis itself. Finally, I will analyse the crisis on the basis of the selected perspective, which is that innovations lead to economic crises.

The Background, Development of the Crisis and the crisis

A credit-driven economy which resulted from the liberalisation of the financial world in 1982 triggered many financial innovations. The internet and the personal computer were technological innovations that greatly contributed to a structural coupling in the global knowledge economy.

---

[25] Reinart and Rogoff (2009).
[26] Schumpeter (2012: 1045).

This structural coupling means that if there are small changes at one place in the global system, these may have serious consequences elsewhere in the global economy; it also means that information travels quickly from one point to another, making it impossible for an individual to understand the consequences of his/her actions in a larger context.

It is difficult to say with any great certainty to what extent the crisis(es) are a consequence of overproduction of goods that cannot be sold at a profit, natural transformation processes, low demand due to the unequal distribution of income, excessive risks taken in a long recovery period (1950–1973) or as a result of other factors. After 1973, there is much to suggest that a downward wave of the economy started, in particular that six smaller economic crises have emerged since then.[27] The difference between the six previous crises and the current crisis is that it is no longer the periphery that is affected, but the centre of the industrialised world. If this assumption is correct, then the good news is that the recession in the long wave, which started in 1973, has bottomed out with the crisis we are now experiencing, and a long recovery period is the light at the end of the tunnel. What will take us out of the crisis, if the assumption that innovations lead to economic crises is correct, are the same innovations that led us into the crisis.[28]

Another feature of the global economy that may reinforce the crisis is that between 1980 and 2006, the wage share of production declined from 67 % to 57 %, and profits increased accordingly,[29] which led to a reinforcement of overproduction, because the demand for goods was reduced. If profits are not reinvested in production, which seems to be the case in 2005,[30] then the crisis is further intensified.

The crisis was not triggered by the fact that the needs of people in the global society are covered, namely through overproduction. There is

---

[27] The Mexican crisis in 1994, the Asian crisis in 1997, the Russian crisis in 1998, the Argentine crisis in 2001, the Dot.com Bubble in 2001 and the "subprime" crisis in 2007 (Sabado 2009: 15).

[28] Here I argue that globalisation, the internet, the personal computer, a modular production structure and financial innovations led to the crisis. Based on the assumptions that are put forward here in the six previous cases, it will be the same innovations that transform and lead us out of the crisis.

[29] Sabado (2009: 16).

[30] Sabado (2009: 17).

much to suggest that it was in fact triggered by a debt bubble, which first manifested itself in the subprime loans in the USA (August–September 2007), as a banking and financial crisis.[31] The crisis spread through structural connections to other countries, for instance, to municipalities in Norway, and countries in southern Europe. The financial crisis was the forerunner of a classic economic crisis, in line with the Great Depression (1929) and the Long Depression (1873–1897). The crisis that began in 2007–2008 is here termed "the Long Recession". The debt bubble has by no means burst, if we consider the developments of public debt in the USA. The USA had a trade and government budget surplus in 2000–2001. However, after tax cuts and involvements in armed conflicts in 2001, they had a deficit of $300 billion in 2002, which has since increased exponentially, and sparked political tension.[32] The Long Recession that started in autumn 2007 is different from previous crises, because of the structural connections in the global economy, which has turned the crisis into a global systemic crisis, with global systemic consequences.[33]

Two innovations that have affected the economic system over time are the development of the personal computer and internet. Although both are inventions that originate from the 1950s, it took 40 years before they penetrated the economy.

Two important institutional innovations changed the world after 1980: the opening of the Chinese market around 1988, and the opening of China to foreign investment. Deng Xiaoping's writings[34] show how his thinking led to China exporting its way to wealth, and how foreign capital was allowed to invest in China. Between 1988 and 2013, we have witnessed the largest economic growth in the world in China; in GDP terms, the Chinese economy was only twice as large as Belgium's in 1980, whereas by 2008, it was the third largest in the world.[35] While

---

[31] Sabado (2009: 15).

[32] Geier (2009: 105).

[33] Sabado (2009: 15).

[34] Deng Xiaoping (1992), Vol. 1 (1938–1965); 1984, Vol. 2 (1975–1982); 1994, Vol. 3 (1982–1992).

[35] Duncan (2009: 46).

this development has taken place, the American trade deficit with China has skyrocketed.

As long as debt-financed demand is possible, economic growth will follow, because demand largely drives production forward, jobs are created, wages increase, the prices of goods rise, and everyone is generally satisfied. Then something happens.

The year 2008 saw the collapse of debt-financed demand, resulting in the crisis of the economic system which relied on it. Economic crises can quickly become political crises, which throughout history have led to systemic crises, where new ways of thinking emerge. Duncan writes: "If our credit-based economic system fails, a geopolitical cataclysm is sure to follow".[36] Duncan's statements are both based on historical comparisons, and foresee a coming disaster. What happens when households are unable to service more loans? It can be imagined that the state takes over the role of borrower, which has partly occurred in the USA. However, what happens when the state is unable to borrow more? In this context, we can see the contours of this scenario by observing what is happening in Greece, Spain and Cyprus today. Duncan is no doomsday prophet; instead, he is showing us how to emerge from the crisis,[37] which the conclusion of this article will also address.

The use of credit is of course not an innovation that first saw the light of day in the year 2000, but dates back millennia. The origin of credit development as an innovation, however, may be dated to the transition from coins to paper money, which occurred as early as in the days of the Roman Empire, when emperors issued notes that could be used to promote trade. We also know about the use of paper money in China in the 800s, when they ran out of copper reserves. What is new is that credit in our times is not connected to a reference standard, such as gold, silver, copper and so on, but only to trust.

Gold was finally abolished as a reference standard for the dollar in the USA in 1968. From 1945, the Federal Reserve had to keep 25 % of its monetary value in gold reserves; before this, it was 40 %,[38] which

---

[36] Duncan (2012a: 169).

[37] Duncan (2012: 27–34, 2012a: 170)

[38] Duncan (2012a: 1).

was an innovation in the development of money. This meant that the Federal Reserve did not have to take into consideration that the amount of money in circulation corresponding to a certain amount of gold in the Federal Reserve. The printing could start on demand, and one can argue that the dollar standard replaced the gold standard.[39]

Between 1968 and 2010, the amount of credit in use increased by a factor of 20. When banks were also allowed to hold less reserves for the loans they gave, this further increased the granting of credit facilities.[40] The next monetary innovation may come with the collapse of paper money, and a complete digitisation of the monetary system, proposes Duncan.[41] This would greatly increase credit opportunities, but could result in serious consequences if "things go awry". However, it must be noted that the credit explosion in the USA has led to prosperity for many, economic growth and new jobs, and also led to significant tax revenues that the government could use in various sectors, such as education, health and the military. Why is the credit explosion so dangerous, as Duncan[42] argues clearly?

What is clear is that this innovation led to, amongst other things, a transformation of the American economy, which involved a change in focus from the manufacture of goods to consumption, service and knowledge production. The ethos in the West became: "Borrow money and become rich". Who can borrow money? In the so-called good old days, you had to save to get a loan. What was new was that you could borrow if the banks thought they could profit on what you borrowed. Eventually the security to borrow became much your own affair, namely your ability to create confidence in the lender. That economic growth became linked to providing credit is one of Duncan's points. If this is correct, why be wary of extending credit facilities? The answer is simple and trite, but relevant: All things come to an end. It's not so much the borrowing that is harmful, but when you can't stop borrowing, which pushes the system over the edge. An analogy in this context is drinking

---

[39] Duncan (2012a: ix).(preface)
[40] Duncan (2012a: 3–15).
[41] Duncan (2012a).
[42] Duncan (2003, 2009, 2012, 2012a).

alcohol: it's not so much the drinking that is harmful, but rather when you can't stop drinking that causes problems. To resolve the problem "the alcoholic" tries to drink a little to get rid of abstinence symptoms; but this rarely, if ever, can be controlled. At one point consumers and states are unable to service more loans—that's when the crisis develops. The point, which Ludwig von Mises realised, is that credit creates bubbles that sooner or later pop.[43] When the credit bubble popped one tried to patch up "the sinking ship" with the use of more credit (as in the analogy of the alcoholic). In the USA, it has been argued that this process goes under the names of QE1 and quantitative easing number two (QE2).[44] Globalisation has also made the metaphor of a sinking ship interesting, because in the case of the global economy, there are few if any lifeboats that can be used when the ship goes down—and if the ship goes down, many will drown. In this case, it resembles a situation in one of Ibsen's plays: the rich suffer loss, the poor suffer from distress. The point here is that there will be many poor and few rich if the global ship goes under. QE3[45] will prevent the economy from collapsing, writes Duncan. The result will be higher stock prices, food prices and initially economic growth. But Duncan predicts that in the medium term, ca. six months to a year, inflation will increase due to the higher commodity prices.[46] New quantitative measures (QE4—?) will prevent depression, and cause stock prices to rise; food prices will also rise. The resulting inflation will be inevitable, writes Duncan.[47] Some argue, however, that inflation is not a problem, because wages will be pushed up by increased production and demand, which is probably correct. However, if wages in China increase, this will result in imported inflation, which in turn, with a high degree of certainty, will lead to pressure on wages and prices in Europe and the USA.

---

[43] Von Mises (1949: 563).

[44] This is a quantitative measure which resulted in money being pumped into the American economy from the Federal Reserve. See http://en.wikipedia.org/wiki/Quantitative_easing (date of access: 15 February 2013).

[45] QE3 was introduced 13 September 2012. See http://en.wikipedia.org/wiki/Quantitative_easing (date of access: 15 February 2013).

[46] Duncan (2012a: 114).

[47] Duncan (2012a: 115–117).

Analysis

In the following I will discuss an institutional innovation: globalisation. Three economic innovations will also be considered. First, I will examine what I term here "modular flexibility", which is an economic, organisational innovation. I will then go on to look at two economic, financial innovations: the dollar standard and a credit-driven economy.

The development of personal computers and the internet are also major economic technological innovations, which have had very serious consequences for the economic crisis that was triggered in 2007–2008. These two technological innovations will not be discussed separately, however. They are included as necessary conditions for globalisation, modular flexibility, the dollar standard and a credit-driven economy; they will therefore be considered together with the discussion of the other innovations in the analysis below.

Globalisation

The structural connections in the global economy were demonstrated in the subprimes crisis in the USA in 2007–2008. It was as if serially connected bombs had exploded simultaneously. In 2009, it was apparent that the housing bubble in the USA took strange detours, reaching large parts of the global economy[48]; the strange detours were the new financial instruments, which were developed by the "rocket science" experts.[49]

Writing about the coming crisis in 2003, Richard Duncan explained why it emerged[50]; he described how when he was on a trip around the Pearl River Delta, from Hong Kong up to Canton, he saw factories all the way along the river as far as the eye could see.[51] This development was one of the results of Deng Xiaoping's policy, which was launched in

---

[48] Konzelmann et al. (2013: 1).
[49] Chorafas (1995).
[50] Duncan (2003).
[51] Duncan (2012: 6)

1980.[52] One of the premises for globalisation was China's opening up to the capitalist market; the other institutional innovation was the collapse of the Soviet Union and the opening of this market around 1990. These two innovations may be understood as the necessary preconditions for globalisation; the sufficient conditions may be said to be the computer and internet.

In short, China's expansion, Russia's participation in the capitalist market and the BRIC countries'[53] economic expansion led to increased globalisation. Globalisation is a relatively recent institutional innovation; although there has been considerable international trade even before the historical period. However, the difference between internationalisation and globalisation, amongst other things, are the two economic, technological innovations, the internet and the computer, which were developed from the mid-1950s. Globalisation is differentiated from internationalisation with regard to the rapidity of information and communication processes. To illustrate globalisation, the following figure may be used: if a butterfly flaps its wings in China, this could start a chain reaction resulting in stormy weather in Europe. The point of the metaphor, which is derived from chaos theory, is to show that the global world is so interconnected that an event in China, such as an increase in wages, can lead to consequences for the production, distribution and consumption in the USA, Europe and the world at large.

The globalisation of the financial markets, writes Soros, was a market-fundamentalist project, which is based on the belief that the market is the solution to every economic problem. He notes that the globalisation of financial markets started as early as 1973 with the investment of petroleum dollars of the rich oil states. This financial market is controlled by the financial centres in the USA, Britain, Germany, Hong Kong, Japan and other industrialised countries.

Duncan wrote as early as the 1990s that he was convinced that globalisation could not work.[54] It worked, however, up until 2008, when the economic bubble popped. In 2003, Duncan wrote the *The Dollar*

---

[52] Xiaoping (1965, 1965a, 1965b).

[53] BRICS stands for: Brazil, Russia. India, China and South Africa.

[54] Duncan (2012: 6)

Crisis; the main point made in the book is that globalisation will result in the continual increase in American trade deficits, consequently, they will be forced to borrow money abroad in order to tackle this deficit. This may be explained by the fact that the USA established businesses in, for instance, China, because it was cheaper and thus more profitable to produce there; the demand, however, came mainly from the USA. In other words, they produced goods in China which they had to import, which led to what Duncan terms "the dollar crisis", or what today is termed the credit bubble in the USA. It must be noted, however, that this globalisation process led to large profits for those who invested capital. However, was this necessarily beneficial to the development of productivity in the industrialised countries, including the US and Europe? Money was made by producing cheaper goods, which was also of advantage to the consumers, and it seemed everyone was apparently satisfied. However, it is likely that this led to there being less pressure on making productivity more efficient than before previous crises.[55] If this assumption is correct, then, many countries in the West may have a productivity problem, which only reinforces the economic crisis they find themselves in.

Duncan also points out in his book that the countries with a trade surplus used this to inflate economic bubbles, which was reinforced by new financial innovations, that is, the new credit facilities that made "everyone into millionaires". Economic growth was thus literally fuelled by borrowed money; demand was driven by credit and new financial credit and investment instruments.

Modular Flexibility[56]

Globalisation, which involves the opening of the market to countries such as, China and Russia, as well as innovations such as the internet and the computer, has led to production being modularised. This involves separating the product into different parts that can figuratively

---

[55] This concerns the Long Crisis (1873–1897) and the Great Depression after 1929.
[56] Johannessen (2009).

be put together and taken apart like "Lego" bricks; of interest in this context is the similarity of Adam Smith's description of pin production to Lego modularisation (1776); however, the Lego modularisation is global unlike the pin production. Modular flexibility is based on the following dominant "logics": the extreme *costs logic* leading to the outsourcing of parts and in some cases whole businesses; the *logic of expertise,* resulting in a high focus on expertise; the *logic of quality* leading to some products being produced where costs may be higher, but where the quality is also higher; the *logic of innovation*, which involves design and product development being done where expertise, design and innovation requirements are the greatest. This modularised Lego logic of the global economy has led to a high degree of complexity and pace of change in the established production processes in the industrialised countries.

The new dominant logic is characterised, amongst other things, by the classic industrial production and work being integrated into global modules. Modular flexibility can best be understood as the globalisation of production processes and the extreme specialisation of work processes with a focus on dynamic core processes. The production, and thus the work, is distributed globally in relation to cost, quality, expertise and innovation logic.

This may result in large savings for companies that outsource parts of their business abroad. The great potential of modular flexibility is related to the reintegration and co-creation of products. It is also reasonable to assume that the market is globalised through an increasing number of products that are available on the global market. In parallel with globalisation, there is also individualisation, which is expressed through a reintegration of the production that takes place when the system of globally distributed modules becomes visible as a product or service. This is done according to a customer and service logic close to the market and the customers. An illustration of modular flexibility is shown in Fig. 7.1.

Globalisation results in the division of labour becoming global, increasing competition and costs being forced down. When labour costs and other costs are globalised, social conflicts increase, which happens because the established wage structures are exposed to global

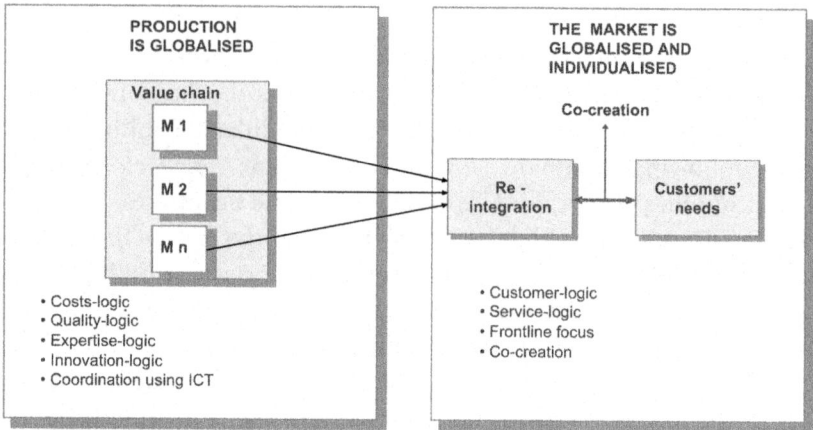

Fig. 7.1 Modular flexibility

competition. Industrial workers in welfare states, where wages and working conditions have been negotiated over a long period of time, and which are not competitive with low-cost countries, are put under pressure by a modular flexible structure. The "economic argument" is that wages over a period of time should not be higher than wages in competing countries.

However, what if this concerns China, and the Chinese wage structure? May it be the case that the argument for lower wages than competitors is wrong? Could it rather be the case that higher wages than competing countries will promote innovation expertise in the home country and thus productivity? If the latter is correct, then the arguments concerning lower wages are fallacious; it is then reasonable to assume that lower wages than competitors leads to lower productivity, and contributes to reinforcing and prolonging the crisis.

Low-cost countries may also include highly skilled workers in their workforce, and are thus able to produce high-quality products. This is the case, for instance, in Bangalore, India. Thus, it is not only the unskilled and skilled labour in industry that competes in the global economy, but also in time highly skilled knowledge workers will face stronger competition. When this occurs, it is reasonable to assume that social and political crises will affect the former industrialised countries.

The Dollar Standard

The USA has veto power in the IMF[57] and the World Bank; thus the USA establishes the conditions for global financial capital, writes Soros.[58] The dollar is also the reserve currency for the global economy,[59] which leads to the "dollar standard" being the actual currency standard of the global economy. The USA can thus increase the credit supply of dollars on a large scale, without this having consequences for US inflation; however, it would eventually affect the dollar's value. In practice, this has led to a new form of protectionism, that is, when the dollar goes down in value, then US exports become cheaper while imported goods are more expensive. In practice, the USA can, as long as the dollar is the global reserve currency, carry out such neo-protectionist policies, without it being possible to rhetorically argue that this is some form of protectionism.

In other words, while gold was the standard before World War I, the dollar has become the new standard in the global economy. As long as currencies were tied to a gold standard, it was difficult, though possible, to "print more money" in the various countries. However, this was far easier once the gold standard was abandoned; then the amount of money in circulation could be increased, for instance, by the USA, by simply printing more dollars. In principle, therefore, the USA could pay its huge debt by printing more dollars.[60] The principle applies, however, only as long as there is confidence in the dollar and the American economy. The more dollars that are printed, the more likely it is that credit bubbles will develop in the global economy. Another effect of the flood of dollars into the global economy is that confidence in the dollar may weaken.

The substantiation of this assumption is that between 1969 and 2000 the total international reserves soared by almost 2000 %. In other words, the global market is flooded with paper money, mainly dollars.[61] The point in this context is that the USA sell their goods in dollars, buy

---

[57] IMF: International Monetary Fund.
[58] Soros (2009: 97; 84–95).
[59] Duncan (2012a); Soros (2009: 97).
[60] Duncan (2012: 8).
[61] Duncan (2012: 7).

foreign goods in dollars and their dollars are invested in various: "dollar-denominated assets, treasury bonds, corporate bonds, equity, mortgage instruments, etc."[62]

When credit is increased, it is reasonable to assume that demand, production and trade increase, and as a consequence a bubble will develop. When the bubble appears, however, it is first measured as economic growth. The inflation that follows from this is addressed by further credit growth; the new bubble created is thus credit-driven. This latter scenario reflects the Austrian economists' views concerning economic bubbles.[63] Sooner or later, writes Duncan,[64] the economy will overheat, and prices will rise more than wages. It is at this point psychological mechanisms are implemented; according to prospect theory,[65] one will then attempt to secure that which has been gained; one of the results is that everyone loses and the bubble pops. It is reasonable to assume that it is at these times politicians and other authorities come forward and speak optimistically about the future. They do this because they know that if people's confidence in the future is weakened, then self-fulfilling prophecies may be established.

The beginning of the depression will probably appear as follows. The spiral that develops will be falling demand and prices, bankruptcies, unemployment and possible financial collapse, at least some banks collapsing. In the same way as nothing can keep on rising up into the skies, then the economic depression will also have to bottom out at some point. The psychology changes. People begin to take risks, rather than defend what they have. When there is no longer that much to defend is the point when it all turns around. What stops the decline and stabilises the economy seems to be when prices and incomes become adequate.[66]

---

[62] Duncan (2012: 8).

[63] Rothbarth (2011).

[64] Duncan (2012: 8)

[65] Kahneman (2011); Kahneman and Frederick (2002); Kahneman and Tversky (1979, 2000, 2000a); Kahneman Slovick and Tversky (1982).

[66] The word "adequate" is used deliberately as a form of precise ambiguity, because no one knows when the adequate level is reached. One can perhaps develop a rule of thumb, for example, how much a house costs in terms of income, 4 – 6 × gross income or the like, but it is not possible to be exact here. The assumption here is when you pay down a loan over 30 years. If house prices are

The "dollar standard", writes Duncan, has made possible an increase in credit, which itself has created more frequent bubbles and pops in these bubbles. The first bubbles occurred in the 1970s, when the USA lent dollars to South America and Africa. This led to the debt crisis in the 1980s in these areas. The crisis came to the Asian tiger economies in the 1990s.[67] After a crash landing in the Asian economy around 1997, money flowed back to the USA as payment for loans, which led to a credit bubble in the USA, writes Duncan.[68]

The Credit-Driven Economy: Financial Innovations

The credit-driven economy is particularly interesting from an innovation perspective. In 2008, there were about "a quadrillion dollars in derivatives".[69] People who had worked on quantum physics in large "rocket science" projects were hired by major banks to develop new financial products,[70] that is, innovations that led to an explosion in the derivatives market.[71] The downside of this innovation is, amongst other things, that the risk in the market has increased considerably, because it is hard to keep track and control the development of these financial instruments. Between 1985 and 2008, the number of new financial instruments and the complexity of these increased.[72]

In 1985, there was almost no one who used these financial instruments, yet by 2008, as mentioned, there were sales of "a quadrillion dollars in derivatives"; then the subprimes crisis struck. The financial innovation was so complex that you literally had to be a "rocket science" researcher to understand them; most people in the financial world are not at this "rocket science" level.

---

more than 4 – 6 × gross income, for example, 10 × gross income, then this may be an indication of a bubble in the housing market (see Duncan 2012: 8).

[67] Duncan (2012: 8–9).

[68] Duncan (2012: 10).

[69] Chorafas (2009: 7).

[70] Chorafas (1995).

[71] Derivative: "A financial instrument whose price, directly or indirectly relates to the market price development of other financial product(s) or commodities" (Chorafas 2009: xvii).

[72] Chorafas (2009: 7).

The ethos of the age's investment logic became trading in derivatives, although few if any understood the risks involved. It all exploded with the housing bubble in the USA. The new financial innovations may be metaphorically understood as financial nuclear bombs, which were serially connected.

In the same way as Japan's economy grew as a result of export-led growth in the 1960s and 1970s, the Chinese economy has grown on the basis of its export-led growth from the 1980s onwards. When the money from the Japanese exports entered the Japanese banking system, it created a credit-driven bubble in the domestic economy. Japan initially tried to invest in other Asian economies, such as South Korea, Thailand, Indonesia and Malaysia. The cash inflow from exports led to an over-heated economy in the late 1980s. The Japanese bubble popped in 1990, which resulted in house prices dropping by more than 50 %, and the stock market by 75 %. Twenty-three years later, in 2013, Japanese banks are still laden with so-called bad loans, and government debt is the largest in the world at 230 % of GDP.[73]

In the 1990s, the US trade deficit with China grew sharply. The trade deficit with Japan and Germany was dealt with by the Plaza Accord in 1985, which led to a controlled lowering of the dollar by 50 % in relation to these currencies. The USA has not the same influence in relation to China. On the contrary, China devalued its currency in 1994, which increased the trade deficit with the USA.[74]

Much of the labour-intensive production in the USA and in the rest of the industrialised world moved to extreme low-cost countries, such as China. The reasons were possibly mixed—there were real economic factors, but also to some extent psychological reasons. However, this contributed to reinforcing the US trade deficit, because they now had to buy the goods from China, which they had previously produced at home. This may be called "the tipping point",[75] which is the point of no return, that is, the point at which a threshold value is exceeded, and the dam bursts; this threshold was exceeded sometime around 1990.

---

[73] Duncan (2012: 11).
[74] Duncan (2012: 13).
[75] Gladwell (2000).

Outsourcing and modular production became part of the everyday life of the big corporations; they could earn more by producing in low-cost countries, because this lowered costs. This led to the US trade deficit exploding around 1997.[76]

The Link Between the Dollar Standard and a Credit-Driven Economy

The new "dollar standard" introduced a new financial innovation—there was no longer a limit to credit. Throughout history, money had been tied to various metal standards, gold being the most common, but now there was no longer such limitation. "Everyone" could borrow money to buy material things, which, amongst other things, contributed to China's export-led growth. Consumers in other countries could purchase more for their wages and loans by purchasing cheap goods made in China and other low-cost countries. The economy became a big credit-driven system.[77] Credit and consumption seem to have been the main drivers of the economy, while previously the focus had been on entrepreneurs and production. In other words, the economic system changed. However, the problem with this economic model occurs when consumers are no longer able to service more loans; that is, there is a limit to how much debt households can service. When this limit is reached, "the tipping point" occurs; something happens both psychologically and in reality. Consumers start to pay off their loans. It is at this time a paradox occurs. The threshold value is reached. The dam bursts, because the new economy is based on credit-driven growth. The dam can however hold, as long as expansion in the global economy increases, while credit is increased by falling interest rates. However, when interest rates and prices fall, this also pushes down wages relatively. In time you will come to an intersection, where the consumer can't manage more credit, no matter how low interest rates are; then you will have finally reached the point of no return, and the dam will

---

[76] Duncan (2012: 13).
[77] Duncan (2012a).

break. Bubbles always pop, sooner or later. The later they pop, the more the bubbles will have developed into balloons, and the greater the consequences will be seems to be a legitimate assumption.

Cheap imports push down inflation and interest rates are kept relatively low. At the same time, there is no clear correlation between credit growth and economic growth in the USA from the 1980s onwards. Duncan explains that credit growth led to increased imports from countries such as China.[78] The multiplier effect for the American economy did not materialise, but was rather transferred to China. In other words, credit growth led to growth in the Chinese economy, but not to the same extent in the American economy.

What has happened in the global economy, according to Duncan, is not only that labour-intensive industries have moved to low-wage countries, but a very large industrial over-capacity has also developed.[79] This is due to the fact that there is a cumulative consumption deficit, because a workforce has emerged in low-wage countries who are unable to buy the goods they themselves produce, says Duncan; he says in an interview: "it's crucial to find a way to increase the purchasing power at the bottom of the pyramid—otherwise the world economy will be heading back to what it was like at the beginning of the industrial revolution".[80] The crisis is exacerbated by the rise in unemployment in the industrialised countries, which pushes down wages in these countries, reinforcing surplus production, price and wage pressures likewise. This is the core of the global crisis we are in, says Duncan. On top of this is the fact that the American consumers, and to a large extent also the European consumers, have prolonged recovery before the crisis in 2008 by various credit facilities. In its consequences, this will intensify the crisis when the balloon pops, is Duncan's assertion.[81] When Americans were no longer able to manage more credit for the purchase of a house or a car, the bubble burst in 2008; one of the consequences was that home prices dropped on average by 34 %. Duncan says the following about this situation: "The

---

[78] Duncan (2012a).
[79] Duncan (2012: 20).
[80] Duncan (2012: 22).
[81] Duncan (2012: 22–23).

only thing that's filling the gap is government spending - that's all that's preventing the US from spiralling into depression".[82]

To avoid financial collapse the US Federal Reserve began a policy of quantitative easing (QE) to boost credit growth; this means that the Federal Reserve, through various methods, provides the economic system with money. QE started in November 2008, to ensure that banks and other institutions avoided collapse; it was expanded in March 2009. In plain language, more money was printed to increase credit. QE2 was launched in November 2010 and lasted until June 2011; it was mostly used to buy government bonds to fund the budget deficit.[83] The government used QE1 to buy up bad loans, cf. Fannie Mae and Freddie Mac. Every QE drives up the stock and commodity prices.[84] Higher stock prices make a positive contribution to economic growth, and some sectors will benefit from higher commodity prices, such as agriculture. However, higher food and oil prices means a loss to consumers. QE is a very important instrument, writes Duncan, to cope with the new depression.[85]

Since around 2011, says Duncan, the disadvantages of the QE measures has begun to overtake its benefits. When food prices rise, it affects people living at subsistence level and the unemployed. He notes that global food prices went up by about 60 % during QE2[86]; and that also the Arab Spring was preceded by a sharp rise in food prices in the region.

The question that may be asked is why the massive influx of credit in the market has not affected manufactured goods to any degree, rather quite the opposite? The answer lies in globalisation. The low wages in the manufacturing countries combats inflation. According to quantitative monetary theory, price rises come when the money supply grows significantly. The million-dollar question is when will the prices of manufactured goods begin to rise as a result of the large money supply in circulation? The paradox is that if the price of rice begins to rise sharply as a

---

[82] Duncan (2012: 22).
[83] Duncan (2012: 23).
[84] Duncan (2012: 24).
[85] Duncan (2009: 63).
[86] Duncan (2012: 25).

result of increased money supply in circulation, this may affect wages and price developments of manufactured goods. The reason is that the higher price of rice will lead to demands for higher wages in China, for example, which will affect costs and thus the price of manufactured goods produced in China. If new QE measures are launched, then it is more likely that food prices will further increase, probably resulting in a rise in the price of rice. One of the likely consequences is that wage demands, for instance, in China, will increase, resulting in higher prices for manufactured goods. It therefore doesn't help matters to make everyone rich by investing in shares with new QE measures, because it will affect food prices, and turn back like a boomerang on the price of manufactured goods. However, there is a time lag before this happens, and it is during this time lag that some people will become rich, for instance, by investing in shares. If the assumption in this part of the chapter is correct, however, then share prices will fall sharply, when the threshold value of wages is reached, for instance, in China, resulting in higher costs for manufactured goods.

Currently, however, US business profits are increasing; in 2012, they were hitting 15 %. Duncan comments that this is possible in the current situation, because labour is getting a lower share. Also, in 2012, corporate taxation as a percentage of GDP was the lowest since 1950.[87] If the balloon bursts, all shares will be unsafe; it's only government bonds that are fairly safe, comments Duncan.[88]

Reflection

The institutional innovations of globalisation and the ethos of the age, as well as the economic innovations, the "dollar standard", the credit-driven economy through various financial innovations, modular manufacturing, the internet and personal computers have evolved into an interconnected holistic system. We can observe in the current crisis a systemic connection between the institutional and economic innovations;

---

[87] Duncan (2012: 26).
[88] Duncan (2012: 26).

a systemic crisis where the structural connections are very dense and complex, and information flows rapidly, has led to this being the first truly global economic crisis. The way out of the crisis can be understood by considering Ernest Mandel's statement: "both a sharp increase in the rate of profit and a huge widening of the market is necessary".[89] Profits seem to come from moving labour-intensive production to low-wage countries. We can find the development of the market in the expansion of the market to the whole of Eastern Europe and China.

"The Commodity Futures Modernization Act" is a financial innovation that led to the deregulation of the derivatives market in the USA in the late 1990s. The value of derivatives contracts[90] in existence increased from $10 trillion to $700 trillion between 1990 and 2012[91]: this represents a vast increase, one which made some people rich or even richer, while the wage share of wealth creation continued to fall.[92] Two-thirds of derivative business occurs between the banks themselves. The scandals in Fannie Mae, Freddie Mac and General Electric, were a consequence of their financial operations.[93] The financial innovations turned the economy into something of a large bazaar, a so-called "lottery economy", where everybody from actors in the private sector to institutions in the public sector, such as the municipalities, and so on, bought a lottery ticket in the worldwide bazaar. In other words, while everyone paid the same price for the tickets, the winnings the various tickets gave were very different. Greenspan called this development an infectious greed.[94] The derivatives market is a good illustration of how the aforementioned innovations have created structural connections in the global market, where there are only a few winners, but many, many losers.

John Maynard Keynes concludes his book *The General Theory of Employment, Interest and Money*, with a claim that is interesting also in the context of the current crisis: "Sooner or later, it is ideas, not vested inter-

---

[89] Mandel (1995: 113).
[90] Derivatives: to gamble on price developments, for example, various agricultural commodities.
[91] Duncan (2012: 30).
[92] Stiglitz (2012).
[93] Duncan (2012: 31).
[94] Florida (2010: ix (preface)).

ests, which are dangerous for good or evil".[95] It can of course be debated whether this is true or not. In the crisis, we are in at the moment, which definitely seems to be "a crisis"—taking into consideration the millions in Europe who are unemployed—then Keynes' statements seem to be of interest. It is the ideas of those who govern and make decisions that affect the development of the political and economic system. If you want to "save your way" out of the crisis, then this will have consequences. If you want to increase the money supply by quantitative measures to recover from the crisis, then this will also have consequences. If you want to increase inflation to get out of the crisis, this will also have consequences. In other words, it's as Keynes says: ideas lead the economy in one direction or the other, and we have definitely not solved "the central problem of depression-prevention", which the Nobel Laureate, Robert Lucas proclaimed in 2003.[96] One of the basic ideas of Keynes, Lucas and Krugman is that we really do not know enough about the genesis of a crisis. We know that different ideas and actions lead to different consequences, but we do not know the basic causes that lead to the economic crises, what transforms these and what leads the way out of crises.

If we follow the thinking of Keynes, then the uneven economic distribution[97] we see in the world today is also one of the reasons why demand is unable to keep pace with increasing production.[98]

It is when globalisation, financial innovations and the two technological innovations, personal computers and the internet, are considered in context, that one can begin to sense the contours of the economic crisis we are now in. It is a systemic risk[99] that becomes evident in the connections between institutional and economic innovations. This means that the global economic system is so structurally interconnected today that one small variation at one place in the system can have catastrophic effects at a different place in the system.

---

[95] Keynes (1973: 235).

[96] Krugman (2008: 9).

[97] Stiglitz (2012).

[98] Keynes (1973).

[99] Chorafas (2009: xxi).

In the decades before 2008, more specifically from the 1980s onwards, the financial markets were liberalised.[100] This led, among other things, to a globalisation of financial capital, and an increasingly credit-driven economy. The numerous product innovations in financial instruments increased in complexity, and reduced the transparency of financial markets. This, in addition to increasing levels of inequality in the distribution of wealth creation,[101] led to an increase in overproduction and the demand for normal goods being reduced or changing in character.[102]

The 1 % of the population that have the best houses, the best education and the highest incomes, have forgotten one important thing, says Joseph Stiglitz, the Nobel prize winner in economics: they have overlooked that they are dependent on how the other 99 % live.[103] Stiglizt argues that the market is not working as it was intended; he also argues that the political system will not or cannot correct errors in the market. This, he says, will lead to distrust of the political system, with unknown consequences.[104] The growing inequality in the distribution of wealth creation is also demonstrated in an OECD report from 2011.[105]

No one, absolutely no one, can say where the current crisis will lead.[106] However, we know that the complexity of the global financial system means that the crisis is global. It is possible that any measures implemented to recover from the crisis will have to be on a global scale. The QE measures implemented by the Federal Reserve have circulated large quantities of dollars in the financial market, which has resulted in price rises for agricultural commodities internationally, as Duncan has shown. Another consequence is that the dollar has been weakened. We have also witnessed a growing currency war between the leading economies, in order to not lose in exports when a domestic currency

---

[100] Konzelmann and Fovargue-Davies (2013: 269).

[101] Stiglitz (2012).

[102] We see, for example, a change in demand for cars in Europe. This has led to vehicle production changing from large to small and micro cars.

[103] Stiglitz (2012)

[104] Ibid.

[105] Konzelmann and Fovargue-Davies (2013: 278–279).

[106] Husson (2013: 119).

rises in value. This may be interpreted as a social mechanism which in its consequences leads to protectionist measures. In other words, one's own exports can be protected by allowing the currency to fall in value, and hinder imports from other countries. It seems reasonable to assume that this form of neo-protectionism will lead to an enhancement and prolongation of the crisis, because it prevents the necessary systemic transformations.

The new markets with their new organisational logic, where modular flexibility ("Lego organisation") seems to be the dominant logic, also increase systemic dependency. It is reasonable to assume that this will initially intensify the crisis, because it spreads faster when the structural connections are strong. In the longer term, this may be one reason why it will be possible to emerge from the crisis, because everyone will eventually see that cooperation is the only way out of a systemic global crisis.

The above discussion and analysis is shown in Fig. 7.2.

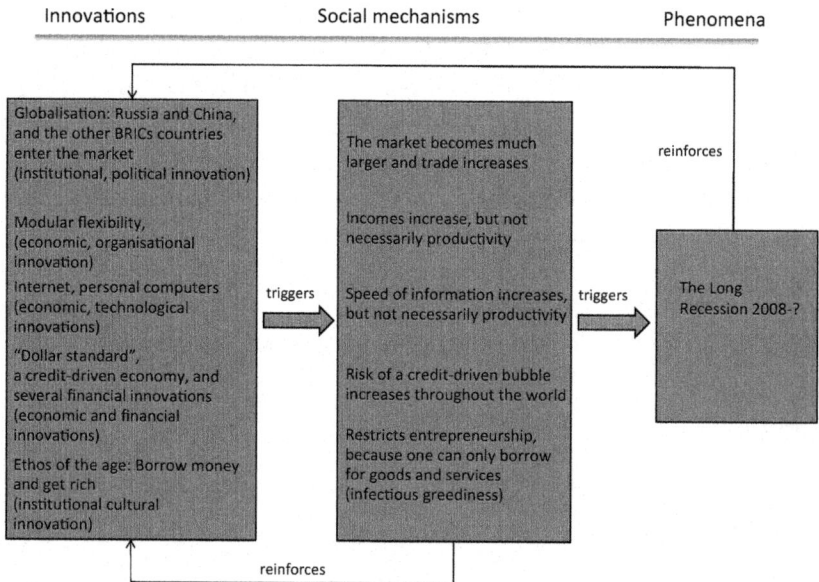

Fig. 7.2 The Long Recession from 2008 to?

8

Conclusion: Innovation Policy

In the short term, economic crises result in the destruction of the old, leading to social crises; but in the long term, they result in increased productivity and economic growth. Figuratively, innovation may be said to have two faces like Janus. The "good face" of innovation exists along a long timeline. The "evil face" shows itself along short and medium timelines, when social, economic and political crises occur.

If the relevance of our fundamental experiences collapses, we will experience problems when using the past in order to explain and understand what is going to happen in the future. Fortunately, we have adequately effective theories that provide us with insight into what may happen, such as Christensen's (2010) theory of disruptive innovations. Briefly stated, "disruptive innovations" involve "situations in which new organizations can use relatively simple, convenient, low-cost innovations to create growth and triumph over powerful incumbents" (Christensen et al., 2003: xv). This suggests that when costs are relatively high, it is reasonable to assume that low-cost innovations will occur. A direct analogy to this is that where real and relative quality decreases, the probability of emerging innovations increases.

© The Author(s) 2017
J.-A. Johannessen, *Innovations Lead to Economic Crises*,
DOI 10.1007/978-3-319-41793-6_8

To reveal how innovations will occur, Drucker (1994: 44) asks the following questions:

1. In which areas of economic life is the real and relative productivity in decline? The answer to the question gives an indication of where there will be major changes, because productivity is the measure of efficiency, and most of the social systems will seek to become more efficient in order to effectively use their resources.
2. Which new knowledge can be transformed into new technology to be used in a market to meet the needs, wishes and preferences of customers, users, patients, students and so on? The time lag between the development of new knowledge, the creation of new technology and the application of this technology in a market takes—on the basis of experience—somewhere between 20–40 years, notes Drucker (1994: 46). The bottom line for companies is to take advantage of the time-lag before the technology is introduced as an innovation in a market.
3. How will the dispersal of innovations affect our market? The dispersal rate of innovation seems to have increased sharply in recent decades. Where the rate of diffusion of innovations increases, it is reasonable to assume that other types of innovations will occur. Among other things, this is because technological innovations in all probability will also foster both organisational and administrative innovations. New technological innovations will also lead to institutional innovations. Therefore, it is important to know where and how quickly the increase in the dispersal rate of innovations will occur.

In Fig. 8.1 we have illustrated where new innovations are most likely to emerge.

Policy Implication for Practice

Put simply, it may be said that innovations evolve in three stages: idea generation, commercialisation and realisation. The realisation phase is often the bottleneck in many projects, not the idea-generation and commercialisation stages (see Andrew & Sirkin, 2006: 5). Andrew & Sirkin

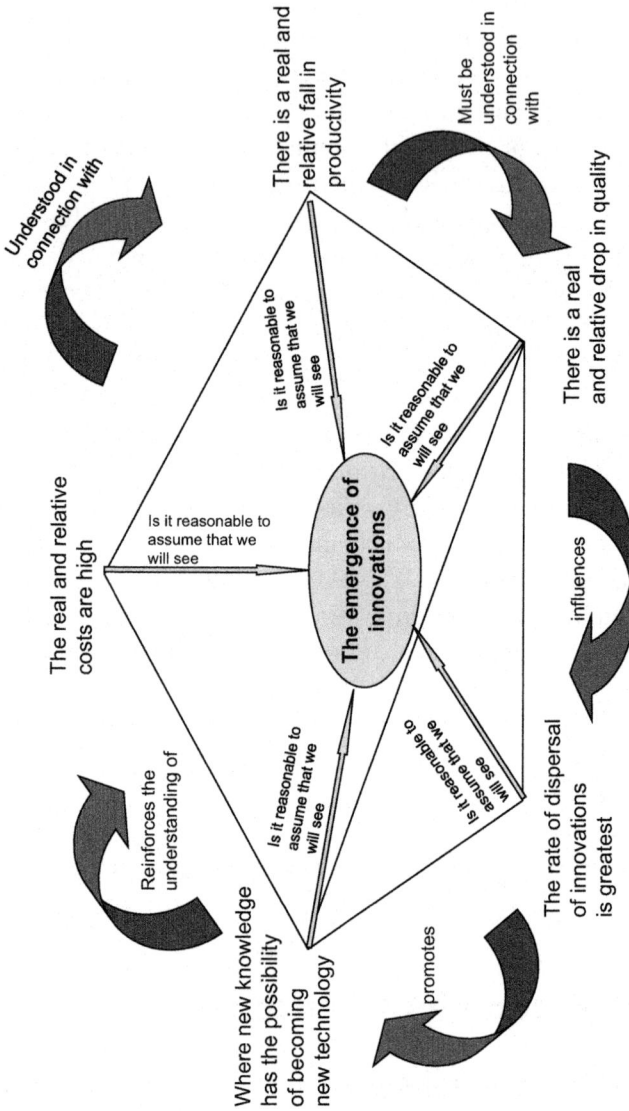

Fig. 8.1 The emergence of new innovations

(2006: 7) term the realisation phase "payback"; this is when the organisation starts making money on the investments it made in the development of the innovation. The commercialisation phase represents the first faltering steps into the market, which often does not reach much beyond the initial launch, rejection and loss.

The innovative leader should make sure to have as many ideas under development as grains of sand in the desert, in order to ensure that some of the ideas reach the market as innovations. The innovative leader should also reduce the time from idea to invoice, and increase the "payback" in the realisation phase. The reason that many fail to come into the realisation phase, say Andrew and Sirkin (2006: 8-9), is that they have not paid enough attention to the four S's:

1. "Start-up costs;
2. Speed to market;
3. Scale, or time to volume; [and]
4. Support costs, or postlaunch investment".

Depending on which processes the organisation has in place, the innovative leader may choose among four main types of models to bring innovations to the realisation phase (see Andrew & Sirkin, 2006):

1. They may take control over the whole process, from idea generation to commercialisation and realisation.
2. They may take control over the whole process, but choose to employ different external actors in various parts of the process.
3. They may take control of idea generation and commercialisation, but choose to license the realisation phase.
4. They may choose an open solution for the whole process, involving customers, suppliers and academia.

The decision on the choice of model will depend on the organisation's capabilities, the product's possibilities for rapid realisation, and the market's receptivity to innovation.

Theoretical Implications

The scope of opportunities that open up at a time when the relevance of our fundamental experiences collapses may be formulated in the following question: How can we gain an understanding of future competitive challenges?

Christensen and Raynor (2003) have shown that by applying innovation theories it is possible to indicate the scope of future innovations with some probability. This in itself is a theoretical innovation; previously, to a large degree innovation was thought of as something that happened by chance, and at best as a result of R & D investment. The pattern that Christensen and Raynor (2003) revealed, among other things, was that businesses that become established "experience a strong incentive to improve, acquire more customers and migrate into high-profit tiers of their market" (Christensen et al. 2004: 29). The result of this drive in the market is that competition increases among new entrants to the market, and between the entrants and the established businesses. Our model in Fig. (8.1) is a development of Christensen et al. (2004), and provides five clear indications of how the emergence of new innovations in the global knowledge economy will take place.

What is the basic driving force with regard to the emergence of innovations? Our answer is that the basic driving force is a shift in thinking. New mental models have emerged as a result of new opportunities provided by new technology. As a result of new ways of thinking and new technology, new business models have emerged. However, they have not emerged from any centre, for example, Tokyo, Silicon Valley, South Paris, the Milan region and so on. There is no centre where one can go to in order to find the solution of the innovation puzzle. Nor is it the case that the periphery has replaced the centre as the driving force in the knowledge society. Indications in the knowledge society suggest that the centre-periphery distinction is no longer viable, because geographic boundaries mean less, and the only thing that sets limits is our mental perception. The relative stability of technology seems to have disappeared. Innovations in every field have become commonplace. The businesses that are unable to develop innovations, or cannot quickly absorb and adapt to new innovations, will be mangled by global competitive forces. This means that innovation leads to continuous and discontinuous changes at all levels and in all areas of society, that is, crises at different levels will occur. One may say that incremental innovations lead to small crises, while radical and revolutionary innovations lead to big crises. There are no unaffected areas, and the crises will occur at all levels. But, if we know where the innovations will occur, we are prepared to what is coming.

As early as 1968, Drucker (1994: 9) called this development "techno-economic catastrophes". However, this is disaster on par with Schumpeter's creative destruction, where something must be destroyed in order for new life to flourish.

Metaphorically, it may be said that innovation leaders are like Minerva's owls: they turn, combine and apply existing knowledge for a market. Classic entrepreneurs can metaphorically be regarded as the parrots of an economy—they fill gaps in the market with existing products and services. Innovators may be metaphorically considered to be an economy's cuckoo chicks, who push aside what already exists. In this way, the cuckoos represent creative destruction, which would not have existed if they had not been protected by those they would later come to harm. New technology enables us to produce, communicate, organise, distribute and consume in different ways than before, resulting in new forms of cooperation. The results of this process include the growth of new ways of working and new forms of management. Future networks will probably be intelligent network-connected systems. We call these networks and their connecting computers "informats", which are a form of collective intelligence in the global knowledge economy. We believe that this collective intelligence will provide the opportunity to bring social systems to a new level of organisation, often termed the "systemic society" because it is interconnected at all levels.

Infrastructure relates to the transport of goods and energy, while the "info-structure"[1] relates to information, communication and knowledge processes. The development of the info-structure means that distance and borders are reduced, geographically, psychologically, culturally and

---

[1] Information structure is abbreviated to info-structure in order to suggest an analogy to infrastructure.

socially. The development of the info-structure has a direct impact on transactions within and between organisations, and consequently affects the organisation of activities within and between organisations; that is, info-structures are the new frontiers in innovation research, and they will help us "see" where the innovations is coming, so we can be prepared for the economic crises which innovation will lead to.

The info-structure concerns the processes that enable the development, transfer, analysis, storage, coordination and management of data, information and knowledge. The info-structure consists of ten generic processes (see Miller, 1978)[2]. It forms the basis of communication processes, and thus also the development of knowledge. The info-structure also greatly contributes to the establishment of new collaborative networks on a global scale. It is precisely the development of a new info-structure that enables new cooperation networks and new organisational and management forms to emerge, such as the focus on the front line and Lego-structured organisations (Adriaenssen, et.al 2016:94-104). While a developed infrastructure enables the transport of goods, services and energy, the development of the info-structure enables the coordination and integration of information resources on a global scale. Social interaction in the knowledge society develops through the new info-structure in the global space, for example, through social networking and social media.

We ask the following hypothetical question: If production and distribution could be 100 % automated, which organisations would grow? The answer would obviously be high-tech organisations, which could

---

[2] Information control, information channels and networks for communication, information collection, information analysis, information strategy, information structuring and systematization, information coordination, information storage and recovery, information culture and information transmission. The ten processes of the "info-structure" may be considered as nodes in a network at different system levels, which together maintain the totality of the info-structure. The purpose of the nodes is to coordinate information in the social systems and networks of social systems, so that social interaction is possible, and new knowledge can be developed. Each of these processes is of strategic importance to the social systems. The control of one or more of these processes results in guiding principles for the control of information, communication and network logic of social systems. Through control of the individual processes one has the opportunity to influence activities in other processes. The various processes have their relative importance in the various systems. At the same time, they are of different importance depending on the system level that is being focused on in the social systems.

allow such automatisation. Obviously, this is only a hypothetical case; nevertheless, the consequences of a development in this direction would be enormous for individuals, organisations and society. The economic, cultural, political and relational sub-systems would be greatly affected. Seeing this coming, will be a way to build up resources to meet the crises which obviously will result from these innovations.

In such a world, policy and political leadership will be more a question of understanding interactive processes and creative actions. In interactive processes, one neither controls nor is controlled. The handling of complexity and chaos grows in such a situation; indeed, these emerge as key dimensions for dealing with the processes that create crises through innovations at individual, organisational and the global level.

References

Adriaenssen, D.J., J.-A. Johannessen, and H. Sætersdal. 2016. Strategic HRM: What Will Work Be Like in the Future and What Impact Will Changes Have on HR Departments? Theoretical Discussion and Practical Inplications. *Problems and Perspectives in Management* 14(1): 94–104.

Aglietta, M., and A. Rebérioux. 2005. *Corporate Governance Adrift: A Critique of Shareholder Value*. Cheltenham: Edward Elgar.

Andersen, E.S. 2009. *Schumpeter's Evolutionary Economics*. London: Anthem Press.

Andrew, J.P., and H.L. Sirkin. 2006. *Payback*. Boston: Harvard Business School Press.

Antonelli, V. 1997. The Economics of Path-Dependence in Industrial Organization. *International Journal of Industrial Organization* 15: 419–433.

——— 2001. *The Microeconomics of Technological Change*. Oxford: Oxford University Press.

Appel, M. 1992. *Werner Sombart. Theoretiker und Historiker des Modernen Kapitalismus*. Marburg: Metropolis.

Archibugi, D., and A. Filippetti. 2012. *Innovation and Economic Crisis*. London: Routledge.

Ashton, T.S. 1969. *Economic Fluctuations in England, 1700–1800*. Oxford: Clarendon Press.

© The Author(s) 2017

J.-A. Johannessen, *Innovations Lead to Economic Crises*,

DOI 10.1007/978-3-319-41793-6

Backhaus, U. 2002. The Economy as a Whole, Seventh Chapter of The Theory of Economic Development, Joseph A. Schumpeter. *Industry and Innovation* 9(1–2): 93–145.

Backhaus, J., and W. Drechsler, eds. 2010. *Friedrich Nietzsche (1844–1900): Economy and Society*. Berlin: Springer.

Bagnall, R.S., and B.W. Frier. 1994. *The Demography of Roman Egypt*. Cambridge: Cambridge University Press.

Balen, M. 2003. *A Very English Deceit: The South Sea Bubble and the World's First Great Financial Scandal*. London: Fourth Estate.

Becker, M., and T. Knudsen. 2002. Schumpeter 1911: Farsighted Visions on Economic Development. *American Journal of Economics and Sociology* 61: 387–403.

Berman, M. 1988. *All That is Solid Melts into Air: The Experience of Modernity*. London: Penguin.

Birley, H. 1992. *The People of Roman Britain*. Berkeley: University of California Press.

Boianovsky, M., and H.-M. Trautwein. 2010. Schumpeter on Unemployment. *Journal of Evolutionary Economics* 20: 233–263.

Brewer, J. 1989. *The Sinews of Power: War, Money and the English State, 1688–1783*. London: Knopf.

Brezis, E.S. 2003. Mercantilism. In *The Oxford Encyclopaedia of Economic History*, ed. J. Mokyr, 482–485. Oxford: Oxford University Press.

Brian, W.H. 1988. *Robert Harley: Speaker, Secretary of State and Premier Minister*. New Haven: Yale University Press.

Butler, E. 2011. *Milton Friedman*. New York: Harriman Economic Essentials.

Callu, J.-P. 1980. Silver Hoards and Emissions From 324–392. In *Imperial Revenue: Expenditure and Monetary Policy in the Fourth Century AD, British Archaeological Report*. ed. King, C.E, 175–254 London.

Carlos, A.M., and L. Neal. 2004. Women Investors in Early Capital Markets, 1720–1725. *Financial History Review* 11: 197–224.

Carruthers, B.G. 1996. *City of Capital: Politics and Markets in the English Financial Revolution*. Princeton University Press: Princeton.

Carswell, J. 1993. *The South Sea Bubble*. Alan Sutton: Dover.

———— 2001. *The South Sea Bubble*, Revised edn. Alan Sutton: Dover.

Castells, M. 2000. *The Rise of the Network Society*. Oxford: Blackwell.

Christensen, C.M. 2010. Disrupting Class, Expanded Edition. How Disruptive Innovation Will Change the Way the World Learns. MCGraw-Hill: New York.

Christensen, C.M., and M.E. Raynor. 2003. *The Innovators' Solution: Using Good Theory to Solve the Dilemmas of Growth.* Watertown: Harvard Business School Press.

Clark, G. 1999. *Betting on Lives: The Culture of Life Insurance in England, 1695–1775.* Manchester: Manchester University Press.

Coase, R. 1992. The Institutional Structure of Production. *American Economic Review* 82(4):713–719. (Nobel Prize Lecture, 1991).

Cochrane, W.W. 1958. *Farm Prices, Myth and Reality.* Minnesota: Minnesota University Press.

Corbier, M. 2005. Coinage and Taxation: The State's Point of View, AD 193–337. In *The Cambridge Ancient History. Volume XII: The Crises of Empire, AD 193–337,* 2nd edn, eds. Q.K. Bowman, P. Garnsey, and A. Cameron, 327–393. Cambridge: Cambridge University Press.

Coulston, J.C. 1988. *Military Equipment and the Identity of Roman Soldiers.* London: British Archaeological Reports.

Cuvigny, H. 1996. The Amount of Wages Paid to the Quarry-Workers at Mons Claudianus. *Journal of Roman Studies* 86: 139–145.

Dale, H. 2004. *The First Crash.* Princeton University Press: Princeton.

Dal Pont, M. 2013. *Business Cycles and Growth Theory.* London: Routledge.

D'Arms, J.H. 1981. *Commerce and Social Standing in Ancient Rome.* London: Harvard University Press.

Dash, M. 2010. *Tulipomania.* London: Phoenix.

De Bondt, W.F.M., and R.H. Thaler. 1993. Does the Stock Market Overreact? In *Advance in Behavioral Finance.*, ed. R.H. Thaler, 249–264. New York: Sage.

De la Vega, J. 1957. *Confusion de Confusiones.* Boston: Harvard University Press. (first published 1688).

Defoe, D. 2010. *Anatomy of Exchange Alley or a System of Stock Jobbing.* London: (publisher unknown). (first published 1719).

Dibadj, R. 2011. Companie des Indes, Governance and Bailout. In *Origins of Shareholder Advocacy.*, ed. J.G.S. Koppell, 169–186. London: Palgrave Macmillan.

Dickson, P.G.M. 1967. *The Financial Revolution in England: A Study in the Development of Public Credit, 1688–1756.* London: MacMillan.

Dosi, G. 2000. *Innovation, Organization and Economic Dynamics. Selected Essays.* Cheltenham, London: Edward Elgar.

Drechsler, W., R. Kattel, and E.S. Reinert, eds. 2011. *Techno-Economic Paradigms: Essays in Honour of Carlota Perez.* London: Anthem Press.

Drucker, P.F. 1994. *The Age of Discontinuity.* New York: Transaction Publishers.

Eichengren, B. 1992. *Golden Fetters: The Gold Standard and the Great Depression.* Oxford: Oxford University Press.

Elliott, J.E. 1980. Marx and Schumpeter. *The Quarterly Journal of Economics* 95(1): 45–68.

Elster, J. 1999. *An Introduction to Karl Marx.* Cambridge: Cambridge University Press.

Erdkamp, P. 2005. *The Grain Market in the Roman Empire.* Cambridge: Cambridge University Press.

Fairlay, W. 2009. *Notitia Dignitatum, Or, Register of Dignitaries.* London: BiblioBazaar LLC.

Fama, E.F. 1970. Efficient Capital Markets: A Review of Theory and Empirical work. *Journal of Finance* 25: 383–417.

——— 1980. Agency Problems and the Theory of the Firm. *Journal of Political Economy* 88: 2–288.

Fisher, I. 1933. The Debt-Deflation Theory of Great Depressions. *Econometrica* 1(4): 337–357.

Florida, R. 2010. *The Great Reset.* New York: Harper-Collins.

Foster, J.B. and F. Magdoff. 2009. The Great Financial Crisis. *Monthly Review Press*, New York.

Francis, J. 2011. *Chronicles and Characters of the Stock Exchange.* London: Ulan Press. (first published 1849).

Frank, T. 2005. *An Economic History of Rome.* London: Cosimo Classics.

Frank, R.H., and B.S. Bernanke. 2007. *Principles of Macroeconomics.* New York: McGraw Hill.

Freeman, C. 1997. *The Economics of Industrial Innovation.* London: Routledge.

——— 2008. *Systems of Innovation.* New York: Elgar.

Friedman, M., and A.J. Schwartz. 1971. *A Monetary History of the United States, 1867–1960.* Princeton: Princeton University Press.

Galbraith, J.K. 1977. *The Age of Uncertainty.* Boston: Houghton Mifflin.

——— 2009. *The Great Crash 1929.* London: Penguin.

Garber, P.M. 2000. *Famous First Bubbles: The Fundamentals of Early Manias.* Cambridge, MA: MIT Press.

Gelderblom, O., A. De Jong, and J. Jonker. 2011. An Admiralty for Asia: Business Organization and the Evolution of Corporate Governance in the Dutch Republic, 1590–1640. In *Origins of Shareholder Advocacy*, ed. J.G.S. Koppell, 129–160. London: Palgrave Macmillan.

Goldgar, A. 2007. *Tulipmania, Money, Honor and the Knowledge in the Dutch golden age.* Chicago: University of Chicago Press.

Gramp, W.D. 1952. The Liberal Elements in English Mercantilism. *The Quarterly Journal of Economics* 4: 467–477.

Hagemann, H., T. Nishizawa, and Y. Ikeda, eds. 2010. *Austrian Economics in Transition: From Carl Menger to Friedrich Hayek*. New York: Palgrave Macmillan.

Hall, T. 2011. Shareholder Activism in the Virginia Company of London, 1606–1624. In *Origins of Shareholder Advocacy*, ed. J.G.S. Koppell, 123–145. London: Palgrave Macmillan.

Hamilton, J. 1987. Monetary Factors in the Great Depression. *Journal of Monetary Economics* 19(2): 145–169.

Harris, R. 1994. The Bubble Act: Its Passage and Effects. *Journal of Economic History* 54: 610–627.

Harvey, D. 2007. *Limits to Capital*. London: Verso.

Hauken, T. 1998. Petition and Response: An Epigraphic Study of Petitions to Roman Emperors 181–249. Monographs from the Norwegian Institute in Athens, Bergen.

Hayes, J.W. 1972. *Late Roman Pottery*. London: British School of Rome.

Hobsbawn, E.J. 1968. *Industry and Empire*. London: Penguin.

Hutcheson, A. 2010. *Four Treatises Relating to the South Sea Scheme and Stock*. London: (Publisher unknown). (first published 1721). (ISBN-13: 978-1170447222)

Hutchinson, T.W. 1978. *On Revolutions and Progress in Economic Knowledge*. Cambridge: Cambridge University Press.

Israel, J.I. 1991. *Dutch Primacy in World Trade, 1585–1740*. Oxford: Oxford University Press.

———— 2008. *De Republiek, 1477–1806*. Van Wijnen: Franeker.

Jensen, M.C., and W.H. Meckling. 1976. Theory of the Firm: Managerial Behavior, Agency Costs and Ownership Structure. *Journal of Financial Economics* 2(4): 305–360.

Jerome, B., R. Cameron, and T.G. Barnes. 1970. *The European World: A History*. New York: Little Brown.

Johannessen, J.-A. 1980. *Industrialisering av torskefiskeriene i Nord Norge (Fishing Becomes Industry)*. Oslo: University of Oslo.

———— 2013. *Innovation: A Systemic Perspective. Kybernetes* 42(8): 1195–1217.

Johannessen, J.A., G.T. Lumpkin, and B. Olsen. 2001. Innovation as Newness. *European Journal of Innovation Management* 4(1): 20–31.

Jones, A.H.M. 1986. *The Later Roman Empire 284–602*. New York: John Hopkins University Press.

Jones, J.R. 1978. *County and Court: England 1658–1714.* London: Edward Arnold.

de Jongh, J.M. 2011. Shareholder activities. Avant la lettre: The Complaining Participants in the Dutch East India Company, 1622–1625. In *Origins of Shareholder Advocacy.*, ed. J.G.S. Koppell, 61–87. London: Palgrave Macmillan.

Kahneman, D. 2011. *Thinking Fast and Slow.* New York: Allen Lane.

Kindleberger, C.P. 1996. *World Economic Primacy.* Oxford: Oxford University Press.

Klein, L.R. 1947. *The Keynesian Revolution.* New York: Macmillan.

Koppell, J.G.S., ed. 2011. *Origins of Shareholder Advocacy.* London: Palgrave Macmillan.

Lambert, A.M. 1971. *The Making of the Dutch Landscape: An Historical Geography of the Netherlands.* London: Seminar Press.

Landes, D.S. 2003. *The Unbound Prometheus: Technological Change and Industrial Development in Western Europe from 1750 to the Present.* Cambridge: Cambridge University Press.

Lenger, F. 2012. *Werner Sombart 1863–1941 Eine Biographie.* Berlin: Beck C.H.

Liddle, P. 2002. *An Archaeological Resource Assessment Roman Leicestershire and Rutland.* Quoted from the following website: www.le.ac.uk/ar/east_midlands, p. 80; www.le.ac.uk/ar/east_midlands_research_framework.htm

Liebeschuetz, W. 1990. *From Diocletian to the Arab conquest: Change in the Late Roman Empire.* London: Variorum.

——— 1992. The End of the Ancient City. In *The City in Late Antiquity*, ed. J. Rich, 1–50. London: Routledge.

Lintott, A.W. 1999. *The Constitution of the Roman Republic.* Oxford: Oxford University Press.

Luttwak, E.N. 1979. *The Grand Strategy of the Roman Empire: From the First Century AD to the Third.* London: John Hopkins University Press.

Mackay, C. 1995. *Extraordinary Popular Delusions and the Madness of Crowds.* London: Wordsworth. (first published 1841).

Magnusson, L. 1994. *Mercantilism: The Shaping of an Economic Language.* London: Routledge.

Mandel, E. 1976/1990. Introduction. In *Capital*, vol I, ed. K. Marx, 11–87. London: Penguin Books.

——— 1977. *Marxist Economic Theory.* London: Merlin Press.

——— 1978/1972. Introduction. In *Capital*, vol II, ed. K. Marx, 11–80. London: Penguin Books.

———— 1995. *Long Waves of Capitalist Development: A Marxist Interpretation.* London: Verso.

———— 1991. Introduction. In *Capital*, vol III, ed. K. Marx, 9–91. London: Penguin Books.

Markwell, D. 2006. *John Maynard Keynes and International Relations: Economic Paths to War and Peace.* Oxford: Oxford University Press.

Marx, K. 1969. Theories of Surplus-Value: Volume IV of Capital. London: Lawrence and Wishart. (original date of publication: 1863).

———— 1976. *Capital*, vol I. London: Penguin Classics.

———— 1978. *Capital*, vol II. London: Penguin Classics.

———— 1991. *Capital*, vol III. London: Penguin Classics.

———— 1993. *Grundrise: Foundation of the Critique of Political Economy.* London: Harmondsworth. (original date of publication: 1857).

Marx, K. and F. Engels. 2002/1976. *The Communist Manifesto.* London: Penguin. (original date of publication: 1848).

McGraw, T.K. 2007. *Prophet of Innovation: Joseph Schumpeter and Creative Destruction.* Cambridge: Belknap Press.

Meiggs, R. 1997. *Roman Ostia.* Oxford: Oxford University Press.

Mensch, G. 1979/1983. *Stalemate in Technology: How Innovations Overcome the Depression.* Cambridge, MA: Ballinger.

Merill, M. 1990. *Reed Smoot: Apostle in Politics.* Logan, UT: Utah State Press.

Michie, R.C. 1999. *The London Stock Exchange: A History.* Oxford: Oxford University Press.

Miller, J.G. 1978. *Living Systems.* New York: McGraw Hill.

Millett, M. 1990. *The Romanization of Britain.* Cambridge: Cambridge University Press.

Morgan, W.T. 1928. The South Sea Company and the Canadian Expedition in the Reign of Queen Anne. *The Hispanic American Historical Review* 8: 143–166.

Murphy, A.L. 1997. *John Law: Economic Theorist and Policy Maker.* Oxford: Oxford University Press.

———— 2009a. Trading Options before Black-Scholes: A Study of the Market in Late Seventeenth-Century London. *Economic History Review* 62: 8–30.

———— 2009b. *The Origins of English Financial Markets: Investment and Speculation before the South Sea Bubble.* Cambridge: Cambridge University Press.

Neal, L. 1990. *The Rise of Financial Capitalism, International Capital Markets in the Age of Reason.* Cambridge: Cambridge University Press.

Nordenflycht, A.von. 2011. The Great Expropriation: Interpreting the Innovation of Permanent Capital at the Dutch East India Company. In *Origins of Shareholder Advocacy*, ed. J.G.S. Koppell, 89–98. London: Palgrave Macmillan.

North, D.C. 1990. *Institutions, Institutional Change and Economic Performance*. Cambridge: Cambridge University Press.

Paul, H.J. 2011. *The South Sea Bubble*. London: Routledge.

Percival, J. 1976. *The Roman Villa*. London: BT Batsford Ltd.

Perez, C. 2005. *Technological Revolutions and Financial Capital*. Cheltenham: Edward Elgar.

Peukert, H. 2002. Schumpeters 'Lost' Seventh Chapter: A Critical Overview. *Industry and Innovation* 9: 79–89.

Rahim, E. 2009. Marx and Schumpeter: A Comparison of Their Theories of Development. *Review of Political Economy* 21(1): 51–83.

Reece, R. 1996. The End of the City in Roman Britain. In *The City in Late Antiquity.*, ed. J. Rich, 136–144. London: Routledge.

Reinert, E. 2002. Schumpeter in the Context of Two Cannons of Economic Thought. *Industry and Innovation* 6(1): 23–39.

Reinert, H., and E. Reinert. 2006. Creative Destruction in Economics: Nietzsche, Sombart, Schumpeter. In *Friedrich Nietzsche 1844–2000*, eds. J. Backhaus and W. Drechsler, 55–85. New York: Springer.Please check and confirm the updated reference Reinert and Reinert (2006).confirm

Reinert, C.M., and K.S. Rogoff. 2009. *This Time it's Different: Eight Centuries of Financial Folly*. Princeton: Princeton University Press.

Rickman, G. 1980. *The Corn Supply of Ancient Rome*. Oxford: Clarendon Press.

Rogers, E.M. 1962. *Diffusion of Innovations*. Glencoe: Free Press.

Rosenberg, N. 2000. *Schumpeter and the Endogeneity of Technology: Some American Perspectives*. London: Routledge.

Rosenof, T. 1997. *Economics in the Long Run: New Deal Theorists and Their Legacies, 1933–1993*. Chapel Hill: University of North Carolina Press.

Roseveare, H. 1991. *The Financial Revolution: 1660–1760*. London: Longman.

Rostovtzeff, M.I. 1957/1998. *The Social and Economic History of the Roman Empire*, vol I, 2nd edn. London: Sandpiper Books Ltd.

Rothbard, M.N. 2011. *America's Great Depression*. New York: Create Space Independent Publishing Platform.

Samuelson, P. 1993. Homage to Chakravarty: Thoughts on his Lumping Schumpeter with Marx to Define a Paradigm Alternative to Mainstream Growth Theories. In *Capital, Investment and Development: Essays in Honour of Sukhamoy Chakravarty*, eds. K. Basu, M. Majumdair, and T. Mitra. Oxford: Blackwell.

Santarelli, E., and E. Pesciarelli. 1990. The Emergence of a Vision: The Development of Schumpeter's Theory of Entrepreneurship. *History of Economic Policy* 22(4): 677–696.

Schama, S. 1988. *The Embarrassment of Riches: An Interpretation of the Dutch Culture of the Golden Age.* Berkeley: University of California Press.

Schubert, C. 2013. How to Evaluate Creative Destruction: Reconstructing Schumpeter's Approach. *Cambridge Journal of Economics* 37: 227–250.

Schumpeter, J. 1934/1951. *Theory of Economic Development.* Boston: Harvard University Press.Footnotes in the references are deleted. Please check and confirm.confirmed

——— 1954. *History of Economic Analysis.* Oxford: Oxford University Press.

——— 1989. *Business Cycles.* New York: Porcupine Press.

——— 2002. Seventh Chapter of the Theory of Economic Development. Trans: U. Backhaus. *Industry and Innovation* 9: 93–145.

——— 2006/1912. *Theorie der Wirtschaftlichen Entwicklung.* Berlin: Dunker & Humblot.

——— 2010a. Friedrich Nietzsche (1844–1900). In *Economy and Society*, eds. Jurgen George Backhaus and Wolfgang Drechsler. Berlin: Springer.

——— 2010b. *Capitalism, Socialism and Democracy.* London: Routledge.

Scott, W.R. 1912. *The Constitution and Finance of English, Scottish and Irish Joint Stock Companies to 1720*, vol 3. Cambridge: Cambridge University Press.

Shea, G.S. 2007a. Financial Market Analysis Can Go Mad (In the Search for Irrational Behavior During the South Sea Bubble). *Economic History Review* 60: 742–765.

——— 2007b. Understanding Financial Derivatives During the South Sea Bubble: The Case of the South Sea Subscription Shares. *Oxford Economic Papers* 59: 73–104.

Shionoya, Y. 1997. *Schumpeter.* Cambridge: Cambridge University Press.

Silvius, P. 2010. *Notatia Dignitatum.* Unknown. ISBN-10: 1142693015; ISBN-13: 9781. 1142693015.

Slicher van Bath, B.H. 1982. The Economic Situation in the Dutch Republic During the Seventeenth Century. In *Dutch Capitalism and World Capitalism.*, ed. I.M. Aymard., 23–35. Cambridge: Cambridge University Press.

Smil, V. 2005. *Creating the Twentieth Century: Technical Innovations of 1867–1914 and their Lasting Impact.* Oxford: Oxford University Press.

———— 2006. *Transforming the Twentieth Century: Technical Innovations and their Consequences*. Oxford: Oxford University Press.

Sombart, W. 1913. *Krieg und Kapitalismus*. Leipzig: Duncker and Humblot.

Sperling, J.G. 1962. *The South Sea Company, An Historical Essay and Bibliographic Finding list*. Cambridge, MA: Kelley Publishers.

Stiglitz, J.E. 2010. Introduction. In *Capitalism, Socialism and Democracy*, ed. J. Schumpeter, IX–XIV. London: Routledge.

———— 2013. *The Price of Inequality*. New York: Penguin.

Supple, B. 1970. *The Royal Exchange Assurance: A History of British Insurance 1720–1970*. Cambridge: Cambridge University Press.

Swedberg, R., and A. Joseph. 1991. *Schumpeter: The Economics and Sociology of Capitalism*. Princeton, NJ: Princeton University Press.

Temin, P., and H. Voth. 2004. Riding the South Sea Bubble. *American Economic Review* 94: 1654–1668.

Tinbergen, J., and A. Kleinkneicht. 1987. *Innovation Patterns in Crisis and Prosperity, Schumpeter's Long Cycle Reconsidered*. London: Palgrave.

Tirole, J. 1982. On the Possibility of Speculation Under Rational Expectations. *Econometrica* 50: 1163–1182.

Tomber, R. 2008. *Indo-Roman Trade*. London: Duckworth.

Tracy, C. 2005. *Henry Bessemer: Making Steel from Iron*. London: Mitchell Lane Publisher.

Van Duijn, J. 1983. *The Long Wave in Economic Life*. London: George Allen and Unwin.

Watson, A. 1999. *Aurelian and the Third Century*. London: Routledge.

Weber, M. 2012. *The Protestant Ethic and the Spirit of Capitalism*. London: CreateSpace Independent Publishing Platform.

Wilson, T. 1948. *Fluctuations in Income and Employment*. New York: Pitman.

Witt, U. 1996. Innovations, Externalities and the Problem of Economic Progress. *Public Choice* 89: 113–130.

———— 2002. How Evolutionary is Schumpeter's Theory of Economic Development. *Industry and Innovation* 9: 7–22.

Zaltman, G., R. Duncan, and J. Holbeck. 1973. *Innovations and Organizations*. New York: Wiley.

Index

Note: Page numbers followed by "n" refer to notes.

© The Author(s) 2017
J.-A. Johannessen, *Innovations Lead to Economic Crises*,
DOI 10.1007/978-3-319-41793-6

173

.

Printed by Printforce, the Netherlands